I KNOW A SECRET

I KNOW A SECRET

*LIFE CHANGING TRUTH ABOUT
THE KINGDOM OF GOD*

DR. RANDY CALDWELL

I Know A Secret
Published By WordView

All scripture quotations are taken from the King James
Version of the Bible.

Published in the United States by WordView Publishing

TABLE OF CONTENTS

INTRODUCTION

"But Seek ye first the kingdom of God, and his righteousness; and all these things shall be added unto you."

Several years ago while I was in Jerusalem, I made my way to the upper room. It is one of the most sacred and special places on the earth. If you have ever been there you know from the time they open the door until closing there is a constant flow of people. This specific day was different. I found myself sitting alone for over forty minutes. Either God blinded me from seeing people as they filed through, or He held them up. Whatever the case may be God used the opportunity to reveal to me deep truth about the kingdom of God. The revelation changed my life. I sorted through the revelation for a solid year because I knew before I could share it I had to understand it.

Before my Dad passed away I had the opportunity to share with him what God had shown me. I can still remember the look on his face. With tears rolling down his cheeks he said, *"Well son, I guess I have been wrong all of these years."* I said, *"No Dad, it's not about being right or wrong, but about God's timing to release the revelation of the Kingdom."*

I am challenging people all over the world to stop "reading into the Bible," and start allowing the Bible to speak for itself. Let's stop getting our theology from hymn books and go back and read the "red print."

This is not another book about religion. I know what religion looks like. I have seen it up close and personal. Religion

1

is nothing more than man's attempt to find approval with a God whom they have never met. Religion is based on rules, regulations, and dogma. It was never designed to give a personal relationship with God. The root meaning of the word "religion" is to *"search."* I am not searching for anything because I know who I am. Religion is man's attempt to somehow find God using his own ingenuity. The creed of religion is *"keep God in a box, so if we ever need Him we know where to look!"* Whether religion is dressed up in expensive suits, blue jeans and a T-shirt, or fancy robes the result is still the same – empty!

God is restoring man to his original position of authority. God's intention from the beginning of time was never for you to just get saved, die and go to heaven. Now, I understand that may go against everything you have ever heard or been taught. Your goal may be to get off this planet and get to heaven as soon as possible, but that is not God's intent. God's original intention was for you to spend eternity right here on this planet.

When Jesus stepped into history His message was not a message of religion, but of the Kingdom of God. He announced it was time to *"repent,"* for the *"kingdom of heaven is near"* (Matthew 4:17). To repent is to change your way of thinking about everything you have heard up until now. When Jesus stepped on the scene He was declaring what was previously unseen was now on the scene (Isaiah 9:6). Jesus declared, *"I have brought the kingdom with me!"*

2

The term "Kingdom of God" occurs four times in Matthew (12:28; 19:24; 21:31; 21:43), fourteen times in Mark, thirty-two times in Luke, twice in the Gospel of John (3:3, 5), six times in Acts, eight times in Paul's writings, and once in Revelation (12:10). The Kingdom is not just one of *many themes in the Bible.* It is common thread from Genesis to Revelation.

God's intention is to colonize the earth and extend His influence through His sons and daughters, citizens, and ambassadors; not slaves, subjects, or employees. Let me say it again – Jesus did not come to the earth to establish religion, or even Christianity. He came to take back authority and dominion that was lost in the garden!

My goal in this book is to show you what God has been showing me about the Kingdom:

- **God's original intent was for Adam to have dominion.**
- **Jesus came to take back what Adam gave away.**
- **For centuries the Church has lived under the veil of deception.**
- **We are sons, citizens and ambassadors of the Kingdom.**
- **The parables of Jesus reveal "Divine Mysteries of the Kingdom."**
- **When confronted by the spirit of religion Jesus was not intimidated.**

3

- **Only those who are "born again" qualify to enter and enjoy the benefits of the kingdom of God.**
- **Money is not the currency of Heaven, but the Earth.**
- **The central question of Kingdom living is "Who is your King?"**
- **And more!**

This book is open ended, with so much more to come. I don't pretend to have all of the answers when it comes to the Kingdom, however, it is my joy to share with you what God has shown me.

Chapter 1

SOMETHING IS MISSING

REVEALING THE TRUE FREEDOM THAT COMES FROM LIVING IN THE KINGDOM OF GOD

I am very concerned about the modern church, the church of the living God. For some time now God has been showing me there is something we have missed. It is my contention that the Church has focused solely on one aspect of the salvation experience, and neglected the greater truth of the Kingdom of God.

It may be a shocking revelation to you, but God's original intention was never for you to die and go to heaven. God doesn't need you in heaven, He needs you here! It's time for the church to unpack her suitcases, and decide that God's divine plan for the church is to impact the world with the message of the Kingdom of God.

YOU'RE NOT COMING OUT OF THE GAME!

I like football, always have always will. The next time you watch a game on television notice when a player gets hurt, or just plain tired he waves his hand toward the bench indicating he needs to come out of the game. You will also notice even before his replacement runs on the field he will be headed toward the bench. That kind of attitude might work well in football, but it doesn't work well in the modern church. For generations the church has been looking toward the bench (Heaven) hoping to be taken out of the game (the world). You might as well quit waving your hand toward the bench you're not coming out of the game until God's purposes are fulfilled!

The "I'll Fly Away," mentality has run its course. The Kingdom of God is not about "flying away" to some distant shore, rather it is about the government of heaven invading and impacting planet Earth. Pure and simple the Kingdom of God is the government of heaven. It is available at this very hour and we can choose to live under the protective canopy of God's governmental system even while we are alive on the earth. We don't have to wait until we die to enjoy the rights and benefits of Kingdom citizenship.

I believe when Jesus told us to pray for God's kingdom to come, and His will to be done *"on earth as it is in heaven,"* he was inviting us to call upon all of the power and the forces of the government of Heaven to intervene in every situation that we face; whether it be financial, relational, or physical.

You may be thinking that I don't believe in the rapture of the church or the soon coming of Jesus Christ. Nothing could be further from the truth, of course I do! That's not my point. My point is we have been so busy trying to figure out how to get off the planet, all the while God is trying to get us to focus **on the planet**. The greatest cure for "rapture fever" is revelation of the Kingdom of God! I don't mean to turn over your religious house of cards, but Jesus is not coming back until the restitution of all things: ***"Whom the heaven must receive until the times of restitution of all things, which God hath spoken by the mouth of all his holy prophets since the world began."*** *(Acts 3:21).* I could be wrong about this but I don't think that has happened yet!

When God began showing me a revelation of the Kingdom my whole focus of ministry, preaching, and just dealing with people changed. It's about the Kingdom, always has been, always will be.

THE REVELATION OF THE KINGDOM WILL CHANGE YOUR FOCUS

There are many Bible scholars who say from the very beginning of his ministry Jesus had a single focus – *"The kingdom of heaven is here."* It is reflected in His earliest teaching:

From that time Jesus began to preach, and to say, Repent: for the <u>kingdom of heaven is at hand</u>. Matthew 4:17

And Jesus went about all Galilee, teaching in their synagogues, and <u>preaching the gospel of the kingdom</u>, and healing all manner of sickness and all manner of disease among the people.

And his fame went throughout all Syria: and they brought unto him all sick people that were taken with divers diseases and torments, and those which were possessed with devils, and those which were lunatick, and those that had the

7

palsy; and he healed them. Matthew 4:23-24

 I think you would agree if you want to know a preacher's focus find out what he talks about the most. If Matthew 4:17 and 4:23-24 represent the first sermons Jesus preached, what do you suppose he talked about? Would it be how to go to Heaven? Hell? Money? Or, maybe how to be a good church member? None of the above! The bottom line is He talked about the Kingdom, which was his focus throughout His public ministry.

 His public ministry consisted of the message of the Kingdom. As a matter of fact he talked about the Kingdom more than any other subject. When you look at the red letter (the recorded words of Jesus) you will see He talked about different subjects, but all were in relationship to the Kingdom. He spoke 70% of the time strictly about the kingdom. He spoke 26% on kingdom finances, and the other 4% on subjects like salvation, healing, deliverance, and the baptism of the Holy Spirit. That means 96% of his message was about the church being financially blessed and operating in Kingdom economics. Only 4% of His message was about other things – streets of gold, salvation, healing, etc. We have taken 4% of His message and made it 96% ours! Don't misunderstand me, the 4% is important, but just not the primary issue. I think we have it backwards, don't you?

 I don't want to get too technical about this but, some writers of the gospel record refer to the "Kingdom of God" while others refer to the "Kingdom of Heaven." The Kingdom of God is "God's rule." It has two aspects; there is a Spiritual Kingdom made up of those who have experienced the new birth by the Holy Spirit, and there is a literal physical kingdom that will come to earth. In the Old Testament you can see the pattern. God ruled His people directly, using the prophets as His spokesmen. (See 1 Samuel 8). God was recognized by Israel as Sovereign, and realized they were "subjects of" a heavenly, not an earthly, king.

This direct rule will once again be seen when the Lord Jesus will one day rule over all the earth. This soon coming event is known as the Messianic Kingdom- the millennial reign of Christ.

John the Baptist proclaimed the kingdom of God to be at hand before Jesus was revealed. Jesus offered the same kingdom to the Jewish people throughout His ministry, which they rejected in Matthew 12. By the way, the "replacement" theology taught today is a doctrine right out of hell!

He focused his ministry about the kingdom and told many stories (parables) with the kingdom of God as the central theme. I want to be clear about one thing – Jesus did not come to the earth to establish a religious empire, but to establish a kingdom, a governmental system that arrived here when He did!

Jesus taught His disciples to pray for the kingdom: In Matthew 6:10*: "Thy kingdom come, Thy will be done in earth, as it is in heaven."* God's will is always present in heaven and we are to pray that his authority will be exercised on earth in the same manner. The kingdom of God is for us to enjoy and benefit

9

from not in the "sweet by-and-by," but in the "nasty now– and–now."

The terms kingdom of God and kingdom of heaven are synonymous. Although these phrases are not found in the Old Testament, they do appear more than 100 times in the four Gospels.

It is seen in the parallel accounts of Mark 4 and Luke 8. John uses the term only twice to describe how one is to enter it. ***John 3:3- 5: "Jesus answered and said unto him, Verily, verily, I say unto thee, Except a man be born again, he cannot see the kingdom of God. Nicodemus saith unto him, How can a man be born when he is old? can he enter the second time into his mother's womb, and be born? Jesus answered, Verily, verily, I say unto thee, Except a man be born of water and of the Spirit, he cannot enter into the kingdom of God.***

Both Mark and Luke use the term "kingdom of God," not the "kingdom of heaven." Matthew used the term the kingdom of heaven when writing his Gospel to the Jews. He uses the term the kingdom of God 6 times. These are not two different kingdoms, the terms "kingdom of God" and "kingdom of heaven" are used interchangeably in the gospel accounts. The "kingdom of God" is used over 60 times throughout the New Testament.

I think one reason we get confused is that Matthew avoids using the term "God," which was reserved, to be used in the synagogues and religious meetings. The Jews in place of saying, "God," would substitute the phrase, "the name."

Matthew, writing his gospel to Jews and aware of their culture, used the term "kingdom of heaven" instead so it would be acceptable, not offensive to his Jewish readers.

The kingdom of God and the Kingdom of heaven are used interchangeably in the gospels. It is only Matthew that substitutes the kingdom of heaven for the kingdom of God. He does use the kingdom of God mostly as an admonishment or warning. He uses the phrase "kingdom of heaven" over 30 times.

Charlie Lewis writing in *The Kingdom System says...* "Most in modern Western society have never experienced a kingdom as a form of government. When we hear the word ' kingdom,' we envision castles and moats and medieval knights riding white horses and carrying huge swords. To us, this is a primitive, ineffective, and outdated system that has little place in our world. But God is not the president or prime minister of the democracy. He is the King. The only kind of government suitable for a king is a kingdom."

In reality, the Bible is a book about kingdoms. It describes two distinct kingdoms, one legitimate King, and one wannabe king. From beginning to end the dominant and constant theme is the epic battle for kingship by this rebel and wannabe king. So ultimately, the Bible is not really a book about religion: it is a book about government. Who will rule this rebellious planet? Which King will you serve? Which kingdom will prevail? From beginning to end, the story of Scripture is the story of kingdom conflict."

When I began to research and discover the importance of the kingdom, I realized that the kingdom involves three things:

1. A King – Jesus.

2. A "Dom" – That's us, who are citizens of the kingdom.

3. Rights, privileges, and responsibilities of the citizens of the kingdom.

In reality, a Kingdom is:

The governing influence of a king over his territory, impacting it with his personal will, purpose, and intent. The kingdom will produce a culture, values, morals, and lifestyle that reflect the king's desire and nature for his citizens.

The Revelation of the Kingdom will establish your Priorities

Jesus said in order for our priorities to be right, we must understand what is first. He outlined our priorities in Matthew 6:33 when He said, ***"But seek ye first the kingdom of God, and his righteousness; and all these things shall be added unto you."*** If Jesus said there is something I have to do "first" what do you think I ought to do first? The secret of Kingdom living is the power of established priorities, with seeking His Kingdom at the top of the list.

What is a priority? According to Merriam Webster dictionary it is..."*Something that is more important than other things, and that needs to be done or dealt with first. The things that someone cares about and thinks are important.*"

With that understanding of the definition then a priority is –

- The principal thing
- Putting first things first
- Understanding what is the most important thing
- Your primary focus
- Putting things in order of importance
- Placing highest value and worth upon
- First among other things

Before I tell you what will happen when the right priorities are established, let me say that living without right priorities will bring total confusion and chaos. I travel a lot. I preach all over America and around the world. Wherever I go I see people living lives of desperation and confusion. Homes are out of order, churches are in a mess, and individual lives are turned upside down. I used to think that these folks just needed to get saved, right with God and everything would be fine. Don't get me wrong, I believe salvation is important, but what is missing is the very thing that Jesus said is our first priority, and that is to "seek His Kingdom, His rule, His Reign" in our lives which will bring order and peace. When His Kingdom becomes our number one priority all of the other "things" will be taken care of by the one who is responsible – and that is none other than the King himself!

Our lives are made up of the decisions we make. They

are usually divided into three distinct categories:

1. Between right and wrong.

As Christians we are indwelt with the Holy Spirit. He is our referee on the inside to tell us when we have crossed the line. In other words, if a Christian is tempted to cheat on his income tax, the Holy Spirit will sound a warning and let him know that is wrong.

2. First things first.

These decisions are based on our established priorities. If our priorities are "seeking the Kingdom first," then my choices are based not just on right or wrong, but how does this affect my relationship to His kingdom rule in my life?

3. Trivial.

Most other decisions fall into this category. For example, "what kind of ice cream should I buy today? Or where are we going to eat lunch?"

The more I preach about the importance of seeking first the Kingdom of God there is one question that seems to stand out above the rest. It is *"how do we make good priority decisions?"* Here's the secret –

Decide in advance that obeying God is the most important priority. Joshua said, ***"And if it seem evil unto you to serve the Lord, choose you this day whom ye will serve; whether the gods which your fathers served that were on the*** *other side of the flood, or the gods of the Amorites, in whose land ye dwell: but as for me and my house, we will serve the Lord." Joshua 24:15*

In light of the decision to obey God first we must determine the true value of things. What are you willing to trade your time for? This may be a shock to your system but every time you go to work you're trading your time for a paycheck. You have determined in advance that the value of your time is equal to the amount of your pay.

There is a story told about a group of thieves who broke into a jewelry store. But rather than stealing anything, they simply switched all the price tags. The next day no one could tell what was valuable and what was cheap. The expensive jewels had suddenly become cheap, and the costume jewelry, which had been virtually worthless before, was suddenly of great value. Customers who thought they were purchasing valuable gems were getting fakes. Those who couldn't afford the higher priced items were leaving the store with treasures.

I think that story is a reflection on how Christians act sometime. We tend to put aside what is really valuable and important in our lives and get distracted with many things that are of lesser value.

"I will place no value on anything I have or may possess except in relation to the kingdom of Christ." -David Livingstone

It is sad to say most people are driven by the wrong

priorities. Years ago a human behaviorist by the name of Abraham Maslow concluded that all human behavior is driven by the same basic needs. *They are: water, food, clothes, housing, protection, security, preservation, self-actualization, and significance.*

Most people trade their time and energy just for the basic needs of life. The spirit of religion is built on the premise that it can meet all of these needs. It goes back for centuries. Religion has to appease some deity in order to secure the basic needs of life such as a good harvest, favorable weather, and protection from enemies. Religion centers on the needs of the individual worshiper! Any of this sound familiar? Churches have become "need" centered and not kingdom focused. God has established His priority at the beginning of creation. And believe me, His order of priority is totally different from man's. His focus is on kingdom rule and kingdom influence on the earth – God says, *"You take care of my stuff, I'll take care of your stuff!"*

It's time for believers to determine that the right order will become a way of life. You and I were created for order not disorder. When proper priorities are established, and order is created our comfort level rises, our productivity increases and stress and agitation are eliminated. Everything you and I are doing right now is affecting order in our life. Even the people you have around you are either increasing or decreasing order. Believe me, the greatest mistake you can make in life is to be busy but not effective. If the devil cannot distract you with an evil ambition, then he will distract you with a righteous one. It's kind of like trying to cut down a tree in your backyard with a hammer!

THE REVELATION OF THE KINGDOM WILL IGNITE PASSIONATE PURSUIT

Personally, the revelation of the Kingdom has changed everything. My ministry, my message, and especially my meetings have been transformed. Where once I would hold a three or four day meeting preaching a different message each night, I now concentrate on a central theme – guess what that is? You're right, the kingdom!

I decided if I am going to seek something I'm going to pursue it with passion and resolve. The kingdom of God must be pursued with passion, it must be understood with passion, and it must be learned with passion!

"Ask, and it shall be given you; seek, and ye shall find; knock, and it shall be opened unto you: For every one that asketh receiveth; and he that seeketh findeth; and to him that knocketh it shall be opened. Matthew 7:7-8

Passion is the intense emotion that compels action. It is the energy of the soul that moves you off of the treadmill of the mundane and mediocre into action. It's the difference between winning and losing, and often between a person who succeeds and a person who fails.

Question: what are you pursuing? If you are not sure let

me ask it this way: where do you spend most of your time? What do you love?

For example, if you love money and that is your first love, guess what you will spend your energy and passion pursuing? Money – of course!

There are many reasons why some people lose passion for the kingdom rule of God in their life. For the sake of space and time let me just name a few:

1. *Sometimes it happens by allowing the precious to become familiar.*

I have been in ministry for many years and I've seen it happen more times than I care to count. I have watched people who had passion and fire for the things of God get frustrated because everyone around them was not as "hot" as they were. Suddenly, those things that were precious became common. It can happen in a marriage, a job, or in a ministry.

"Familiarity paints our homes with drabness. It replaces evening gowns with bathrobes, nights on the town with the evenings in the recliner, and romance with routine. It scatters the dust off of yesterday over the wedding pictures until they become a memory of another couple in another time." Max Lucado

2. *Sometimes it happens by allowing the acceptance and approval of men to be more important than the passionate pursuit of the kingdom of God.*

We are living in an RC (religiously correct) environment. It's the idea of just fitting in, being normal, just plain average. After all, no one wants to stand out from the crowd right? So, what do we do? We turn down the temperature of our passion and slowly fade back into the environment of our religious surroundings where we can sit comfortably on Sunday morning. It's easy to shout Amen and Hallelujah knowing nothing will be accomplished, and we are no threat to the devil.

3. *Sometimes it happens because we live with false expectations.* Sometimes we don't have passion for the kingdom of God because our expectations are not realistic. Living with false expectations can be a "passion killer."

If I had to list the number one false expectation it would be the idea that "I'll always live on the mountaintop, and never experience the valley." It is unrealistic to think that we will never have times and seasons when things and circumstances are "not so hot." Of course, the ultimate desire is to stay on fire 24/7. We all have highs and lows, why? First of all because we are human, and second because life has a way of showing up with some unusual and trying circumstances that even the most Holy Ghost anointed Christian has difficulty dealing with.

TIME TO DECIDE

Will you seek the revelation of the kingdom with focus and passion? If you are going to seek the kingdom your desire for revelation will have to exceed your present level of understanding. I know when I say that in some churches I get some very strange looks because many people have yet to understand the importance of "seeking first the kingdom of God, and His righteousness."

There will be opposition when you determine to move out of your comfort zone to seek His kingdom at all cost. In the next chapter I am going to show you there are two kingdoms in operation. Two kingdoms are about to collide, so you might want to strap your seatbelt a little tighter – things are about to get bumpy!

Chapter 2

WHEN KINGDOMS COLLIDE

But seek ye first the kingdom of God, and his righteousness; and all these things shall be added unto you. -Matthew 6:33

If Jesus spent His entire public ministry preaching the gospel of the Kingdom, then why don't we hear more of it today? You would think the shelves of the local Christian bookstores would be filled with volumes about the Kingdom of God. The last time I looked I could only find a few volumes that made any sense. It's puzzling to me. There just isn't a polite way to say it, so I will just go ahead and say it – *for the most part the church is infected with the spirit of dumb when it comes to kingdom revelation!* So is it any wonder why the modern church spends more time worrying about the color of the carpet, or the next bake sale than following the clear mandate of Jesus to make disciples of all nations? We haven't missed it by mile, we have missed it by light years!

In Matthew 6, He told us to seek the Kingdom first. The topic of "The Kingdom" was the theme throughout His parables. His public message (The red letter) was always about the Kingdom. Remember, I told you that 70% of his teaching was about the kingdom, 26% on kingdom finances, and only 4% on subjects like salvation, healing, deliverance, and the baptism of the Holy Spirit. That's not to say that we should not teach about the 4%, because those issues are important, but just not MOST important.

Keep in mind, when He taught about the Kingdom He was not referring to the Kingdom of Heaven. The Kingdom of heaven is a geographical location. It has New Jerusalem as her capital city, with streets of gold and walls of Jasper. The Kingdom of God is a system of government, and dominion that Adam threw away over 4,000 years ago.

There are over one hundred fifty references Jesus made to the "Kingdom" in the New Testament. When He taught us how to pray, He included the phrase "...**Thy Kingdom come.**"

OPEN YOUR EARS TO HEAR, AND YOUR HEARTS TO UNDERSTAND

The revelation of the kingdom has always been available to those who have experienced the new birth. But you say, *"Brother Randy, if that's true why don't we hear it every time we go to church?"* Why aren't more people talking about it? I'm glad you asked!

You see my friend, you and I have all the tools necessary to "search out" the truth of God's word. Paul told Timothy to... ***"Study to shew thyself approved unto God, a workman that needeth not to be ashamed, rightly dividing the word of truth (2 Timothy 2:15).*** When your desire lines up with a willingness to search out the truth, God will reveal it to you. Whatever you are hungry for God will see to it that you get it. Even if you are hungry for nothing!

I can prove that statement with Scripture. Proverbs 25:2

says: ***"It is the glory of God to conceal a thing: but the honour of kings is to search out a matter."*** When you read the English translation of that verse different words are used to describe the same thing. When you search out the meaning a burst of revelation will hit you.

The words *"glory"* and *"honor"* are the same words in the Hebrew. It is the word *"kabod."* It literally means *"the splendor, benefit and reputation of God to conceal a thing, but it is the splendor, benefit, and reputation of kings to search out the matter."*

The words *"thing"* and *"matter"* are also the same. It is the Hebrew word, *"Dabar."* It means *"a word inside of a word that is put there to be searched out."*

So far, the literal translation of Proverbs 25:2 reads like this: *"It is the splendor, benefit, and reputation of God to conceal a word inside of a word to be hid until the proper time to be revealed. It is the splendor, benefit, and reputation of Kings to search out the word God has put inside the word."*

Who are the kings? The Hebrew root word is "Malak." In that form it is only found 3 times in the Bible. It does not mean those who are reigning now, but those who are appointed to reign in the future. ***Revelation 1:5-6 declares: "And from Jesus Christ, who is the faithful witness, and the first begotten of the dead, and the prince of the kings of the earth. Unto him that loved us, and washed us from our sins in his own blood, and hath made <u>us kings and priests</u> unto God and his Father; to*** *him be glory and dominion for ever and ever. Amen.*

Now *Proverbs 25:2* reads: "*It is the splendor, benefit, and reputation of God to conceal (to hide, to provoke someone to search out) a word inside of a word to be hid until the proper time to be revealed. It is the splendor, benefit, and reputation of Kings, those who have been appointed to reign in the future, to search out the word God has put inside the word that has previously been hid until the time appointed!*"

God's desire is for you and me to seek truth. When you seek, guess what will happen? That's right, you will find. When you knock it will be opened, and if you ask you shall receive. Showing up at church once a week, or scanning the Bible for a verse when you get in trouble will not give you Kingdom revelation. Gold does not fall out of the tree and hit you in the head when you need a little extra money. You have to search for it with diligence, and a little sweat! Likewise, you will never receive golden nuggets of revelation from the Bible without the same effort.

It is clear that Jesus recognized another kingdom, and these two kingdoms are in conflict with one another.

Jesus successfully endured temptation from the devil... **"Again, the devil taketh him up into an exceeding high mountain, and sheweth him all the kingdoms of the world, and the glory of them; And saith unto him, All these things will I give thee, if thou wilt fall down and worship me. Matthew 4:8-9:** He was saying*; "All of it can be yours."* He

24

declared that he had control over the kingdoms of this world...
And the devil said unto him, All this power will I give thee, and the glory of them: for that is delivered unto me; and to whomsoever I will I give it. Luke 4:6

Do you think Satan was able to give these kingdoms of the world to Jesus? In **John 12:32**, Jesus referred to Satan as ...*the ruler of this world.* In **2 Corinthians 4:4**, the apostle Paul refers to him as ...*the god of this world.* In **Ephesians 2:2** he is described as... *"the prince of the power of the air."*

That was partly true, but it was a great lie also. There is indication that he has temporary control now, but he could not grant permanent control. Remember, everything the devil can offer you is only temporary. It will not bring any lasting satisfaction.

Satan is a created being, a creature; but he wanted to be worshiped and served like God. This attitude led him to rebel against God and seek to establish his own kingdom. (Isaiah 14:12-14). Jesus exposed Satan and his tactics, and He defeated him. Because of His victory, we can have victory over the tempter. Satan desired worship and service, and it is obvious from Scripture that Jesus Christ would give him neither!

WHICH KINGDOM DO YOU OPERATE IN?

The conflict between these two kingdoms started early in the ministry of Jesus, and continued all the way through to the cross.

Jesus established there are two kingdoms in operation:

1. The kingdom of light.

Although there are different words used for "light" in the New Testament, when the Bible talks about the *kingdom of light it is talking about the kingdom of knowledge.* It not only refers to knowledge, but to government, kingdom authority, and dominion.

2. The kingdom of darkness.

Again, there are many words used to describe darkness, but when referring to the *kingdom of darkness* it literally means "ignorance." To live and operate in the kingdom of darkness or ignorance is to be unlearned, without knowledge or information about the kingdom of light.

The devil's plan is to keep you in darkness (ignorance). He doesn't care how much you shout or speak in tongues. It doesn't matter to him if you lay hands on the sick. He could care less if you show up to church every time the doors are open. What he doesn't want you to have is light, or knowledge about the kingdom of God! He knows when you do, you become a threat to the kingdom of darkness, and he will do everything possible to stop you. The point is there are two kingdoms on the same planet. There will always be confrontation and conflict between the two. They are diametrically opposed.

You see, when you gain information it will bring knowledge. Knowledge always brings understanding.

Understanding will unlock trust and trust will release faith. When you gain knowledge and understanding about God you can trust Him. You can trust that He is not out to "get you," but has your best interest at heart. Once you know that, you can release your faith to walk in kingdom dominion!

SO, WHAT DOES THE "WORLD" OF DARKNESS REALLY MEAN?

In the high priestly prayer of Jesus in John 17 He refers to the relationship of the believer to the world. According to Jesus the child of God has been saved out of the world's system. You haven't been patched up, no, you are a brand-new creation. You have a new nature, a firm destiny and a new citizenship (See John 17; Philippians 3). You now have all rights and privileges of a King's Kid. With royal blood flowing through your veins you have the right to walk in kingdom revelation, exercise dominion over the evil one, and live above your circumstances not beneath them!

CAUTION!

The apostle John warns the believer about any emotional tie to the very place he was rescued from – what is that? The world's system: *Love not the world, neither the things that are in the world. If any man love the world, the love of the Father is not in him. 1 John 2:15*

When the apostle John uses the word "world" he is not talking about the world of creation. The Bible makes it very clear that ***"The God who made the world and everything in it is the Lord of heaven and earth, and does not live in temples built by human hands" (See Acts 17:24).*** Nor, is he talking about the world of lost humanity. Jesus loved the world of lost men so much that he gave himself as a sacrifice to redeem it (See John 3:16; 1 Peter 1:18).

The word for "world" that both Jesus and John used is the Greek word *"kosmos."* Strong's Concordance gives the definition as: *the world, universe; worldly affairs; the inhabitants of the world; adornment. An "ordered system" (like the universe, creation).*

The English words "cosmopolitan" or "cosmic" derive from the Greek word *"kosmos."* Another derivative is our English word "cosmetic." You don't have to be a brain surgeon to figure out that "cosmetic" means to "put things in proper order, or to arrange things as they should be." If you're not sure about the meaning just ask any woman the next time you see her putting on her makeup!

The world that John is referring to is a "system" or a pattern of thought, and behavior that is operating in total darkness (ignorance) apart from the kingdom of God which is knowledge and light.

We use the same word "world" in the sense of a system in our daily conversation. When you turn on the radio and the announcer says, "Now news from the world of sports," he is not referring to some planet out in the universe where they play sports." At least, I hope you don't think that is what he's talking about. No, he is talking about an organized system, made up of certain activities, rules and regulations where people with the same ideas and set of values play sports. The same would be true when speaking about "the world of politics." In other words, behind what we see, is an invisible arrangement of things (system) that we cannot see. It is that system that keeps things moving forward.

There are 3 things I need you to know about the "world's system" that are totally opposed to the Kingdom of God:

1. The world's system is controlled by its own Ruler.

Jesus identified Satan as "the prince of this world." Satan has an organization of evil spirits (Ephesians 6:11-12) working with him and influencing the affairs of this world.

"Now is the judgment of this world: now shall the prince of this world be cast out." John 12:31

In whom the god of this world hath blinded the minds of them which believe not, lest the light of the glorious gospel of Christ, who is the image of God, should shine unto them. 2 Corinthians 4:4

2. The world's system is inhabited by its own children.

The Bible makes it clear the lost, or unsaved are a part of the *"children of this world."* They may even attend church, and act religious. But, the fact is they do not know or understand the things of God. Just by going to church doesn't mean you are a believer any more than hanging around in a garage makes you an automobile! The tragic truth is the "children of this world" will either willingly or unwillingly be used by the devil to fulfill his purposes. They are constantly energized by the "prince of the power of the air."

And you hath he quickened, who were dead in trespasses and sins; Wherein in time past ye walked according to the course of this world, according to the prince of the power of the air, the spirit that now worketh in the children of disobedience: Among whom also we all had our conversation in times past in the lusts of our flesh, fulfilling the desires of the flesh and of the mind; and were by nature the children of wrath, even as others. Ephesians 2:1-3

3. The world's system even has its own brand of perverted wisdom.

All you have to do is turn on the television and you will see the wisdom of this world is totally upside down. I don't mean to upset you, but if you are depending on worldly wisdom to teach you how to live, train your children, or succeed in business you are in for a shocking revelation. Worldly wisdom is the polar opposite of the kingdom of light which is necessary to live a life that is pleasing to God. Something that irritates me beyond words is someone writing a book on how to raise (train) your child and they don't even have children themselves!

Simon Peter said the world system is corrupt through its lust (2 Peter 1:4). How corrupt is its wisdom?

Let me give you an example: The law says you can terminate the life of a baby while he/she is still in her mother's womb, and in some cases even up until the last trimester. If you really want to be upset read about the horrific procedure called partial-birth abortion.

But, the law also says, if the baby is born, and is outside the womb and you kill it, it's called murder. So, let me get this straight – it's all right to kill the baby as long as it's inside the womb – but once outside the womb its murder! *Now, you say Brother Caldwell that makes no sense at all, that is the dumbest thing I've ever heard. You know what? I agree with you one hundred percent, but that is what demonic, worldly wisdom looks like.*

Howbeit we speak wisdom among them that are perfect: yet not the wisdom of this world, nor of the princes of this world, that come to nought: But we speak the wisdom of God in a mystery, even the hidden wisdom, which God ordained before the world unto our glory: Which none of the princes of this world knew: for had they known it, they would not have crucified the Lord of glory. 1 Corinthians 2:6-8

Who is a wise man and endued with knowledge among you? let him shew out of a good conversation his works with meekness of wisdom. But if ye have bitter envying and strife in your hearts, glory not, and lie not against the truth. This wisdom descendeth not from above, but is earthly, sensual, devilish. For where envying and strife is, there is confusion and

31

every evil work. But the wisdom that is from above is first pure,
then peaceable, gentle, and easy to be intreated, full of mercy
and good fruits, without partiality, and without hypocrisy.
James 3:13-17

Jesus did not leave heaven to die on a cross so that you could escape hell and go to heaven. His purpose was not to endure such physical agony so that you could just "get by." NO! The divine rescue mission was to break you free from the dominion of an evil world system, and give you dominion OVER that very system!

When you were saved, born from above, the greatest rescue mission ever conceived in the mind of man took place. Needless to say more happened to you than just getting your ticket punched for heaven.

Rescued from what? Darkness – ignorance – the present evil world – the power of the evil one:

But ye are a chosen generation, a royal priesthood, an holy nation, a peculiar people; that ye should shew forth the praises of him who hath called you out of <u>**darkness into his marvellous light**</u>*; 1 Peter 2:9*

Who gave himself for our sins, that he might **deliver** *(Rescue) us from this present evil world, according to the will of God and our Father: Galatians 1:4*

When Paul wrote about being rescued he was not talking about something he heard in Sunday school or read in a book. He wrote from personal experience. When Jesus knocked him off of his donkey into the dust on the road to Damascus Paul was rescued from the darkness of legalism, and the straitjacket of man-made traditions. The light of the glory of Jesus was so bright it blinded Paul for several days, yet for the first time in his life he could see! He was given a new purpose, a new name, and a new reason to live.

It was an experience that Paul never got over. Whether he was speaking to a group of leaders, ordinary church folk, or governors and Kings he could never stop talking about being rescued and set free from the world of darkness!

He talked about it again in Colossians:

Who hath **delivered (Rescued***) us from the power of darkness, and hath translated us into the kingdom of his dear Son: In whom we have redemption through his blood, even the forgiveness of sins: Who is the image of the invisible God, the firstborn of every creature: Colossians 1:13-15*

For me the first part of Paul's statement (Verse 13) is enough to make you want to shout!

He states*: We have been "delivered" or rescued from the "power" of darkness*. The word "power" is the Greek word "exousia" which means in this context: *"authority, delegated power, tyranny, unrestrained lawlessness or arbitrary power."* The expression "the power of darkness" also is found in Luke

33

22:53, where again it is the idea of disorder.

We have been "translated" through the new birth experience from the kingdom of darkness and disorder to the kingdom of light. The phrase *"translated us"* is a phrase used to describe the deportation of a population from one country into another. Jesus Christ did not redeem us from the bondage and power of the kingdom of darkness to wander aimlessly in the world. Just as God delivered Israel from the bondage of Egypt and took them into the Promised Land (inheritance) so God brings us out that he might bring us into our land of promise.

The literal translation of verse 13 reads like this*: "Who delivered us out of the tyrannical rule of the darkness and transferred us into the kingdom of the son of his love." To which I say* **HALLELUJAH!**

The Church has been walking around under the veil of deception for centuries. It is the greatest deception known to man. You will have to turn the page to find out what that is. But, I have to warn you things are about to get messy!

Chapter 3

THE GREAT DECEPTION

Let no man deceive himself. If any man among you seemeth to be wise in this world, let him become a fool, that he may be wise. 1 Corinthians 3:18

It is a biblical fact when God gets ready to move an individual to the next level of revelation He will send someone in your life to buffet you. And, more than likely you will be offended more than you will be thrilled.

Likewise, when the devil wants to mess us up he will also put someone in our life. The key is to learn the difference between a John and a Judas. Both men had a close relationship to Jesus. One laid his head on Christ bosom, while the other kissed his cheek. One intended to worship, while the other intended to kill. It's imperative for you and me to learn the difference between the two!

I guess you could say my goal is to be the individual to challenge your traditional thinking about the Kingdom of God, the real mission of the church, and our identity in Christ. We have been sub-normal for so long that to be a normal Holy Ghost filled child of the King looks like we are abnormal. I don't know about you but I choose to be abnormal every day of the week and twice on Sunday!

I am determined to get the revelation of the Kingdom into you even at the risk of offending you. I certainly wouldn't classify myself as the Apostle John, but believe me I am certainly

35

not Judas. I am just a preacher that God's chosen to use as "Holy Ghost sandpaper" to the body of Christ. Remember, the Holy Ghost will challenge you to make you better. The enemy will challenge you to live in doubt, fear, and confusion. If you have an ounce of discernment you can tell the difference between the two.

You may say, *"Brother Caldwell are you about to take a sledgehammer and knock down a few theological idols?"* I guess my reply would be, *"Let the pounding begin!"*

GOD'S ORIGINAL INTENTION – WAS NOT RELIGION

The original plan of mankind was not for us to have religion. The original plan of mankind was not for us to come together and have praise and worship and preaching. If you go back to the Garden of Eden, before the fall, you will see there was relationship and intimacy with the Father. Religion was unheard of. It was not needed because Adam and Eve lived in a perfect environment.

When God created man it was the supreme act of creation. Why? He wanted someone to share in His authority and rule, not be just a slave or a servant. According to Strong's definition the garden Eden means "the Garden of delight." Think about that for a moment. God made man in his image, prepared a perfect place that was ideal and pleasant, and filled it with his presence!

And God said, Let us make man in our image, after our likeness: and let them have dominion over the fish of the sea, and over the fowl of the air, and over the cattle, and over all the earth, and over every creeping thing that creepeth upon the earth. So God created man in his own image, in the image of God created he him; male and female created he them. And God blessed them, and God said unto them, Be fruitful, and multiply, and replenish the earth, and subdue it: and have dominion over the fish of the sea, and over the fowl of the air, and over every living thing that moveth upon the earth. Genesis 1:26-28

Religion is based on rules, regulations, and dogma. It was never designed to give a personal relationship with God. The root meaning of the word "religion" is to *"search."* I am not searching for anything because I know who I am. Religion is man's attempt to somehow find God using his own ingenuity. It may be dressed up in fancy robes but the result is still the same – empty!

If you have ever heard me preach for more than five minutes you know I have an incredible disdain for the spirit of religion. Religion stinks to high heaven! I am not talking about folks gathering together on Sunday to worship, sing and praise God. That is a good thing. But, you have to understand that religion is nothing more than a man-made club put together to fill the void. To search for something it cannot give – a one– on –one relationship with the one who created you.

GOD'S ORIGINAL INTENTION – WAS NOT FOR YOU TO GO TO HEAVEN!

God wanted to expand the kingdom of Heaven to the Kingdom here on this earth ruled by beings He called mankind. He wanted His Kingdom on earth to be an extension of the Kingdom of Heaven. Therefore, He wanted His "seen" Kingdom to be ruled by His presence from the "unseen" Kingdom. In other words He wanted this seen Kingdom to be ruled by the unseen Kingdom through the unseen spirit of Christ that is in the "seen" body on the scene!

We are in the realm of the Kingdom of God and God wants us to conduct business for His Kingdom that is unseen by the natural eye. We are His mouthpiece those of us that are here on the scene and we are created to dominate this planet! His intention is for us to rule – not be ruled. To dominate, not be dominated.

God's intention from the beginning of time was never for you to be in heaven. Now I understand that goes against everything you have ever heard or been taught. Your goal may be to get off this planet and get to heaven as soon as possible, but that is not God's goal. God's original intention was for you to spend eternity right here on this planet.

"Well, Brother Caldwell, I don't know about all of that, I just want to go to heaven." If that is your intention I have good news and bad news for you. The good news is if you die before the rapture you are going to go to heaven. But, for those who

38

think that's all there is I have a bit of unsettling news; you're not going to stay there. God does not want you to be out there wandering somewhere in eternity in what we commonly refer to as heaven. God wants you here on this mud ball called planet Earth. But, the good news is when the rapture takes place those that are ready (those who are born again) are going. But, after seven years (as it's been taught), all the saints who have died previously along with all the raptured Saints are coming back here to this planet for eternity to rule and reign with Christ. Many have asked me, *"Brother Caldwell, are you pre-trib, mid-trip, or post-trib."* My answer is the same every time – *"I don't give a rip –trib, because no matter when He comes I want to be ready!"*

JESUS DID NOT COME TO ESTABLISH A RELIGION.

This may upset you, but Jesus did not come to earth to: live a sinless life, die on the cross as the perfect sacrifice for sin; be buried in a borrowed tomb; rise from the dead; teach His disciples for 40 days after the resurrection; ascend back to heaven; leave a promise to return just to *ESTABLISH A RELIGION CALLED CHRISTIANITY!* He came to establish a Kingdom. His intent was to take back what Adam gave away to the Devil. He did not leave heaven to bring us just another religion so theologians could speculate about certain doctrines, which in itself produces nothing more than endless arguments and conflict.

God designed us to live in freedom under His

government not under the bondage of the kingdom of darkness. As *"the way, the truth, and the life"* Jesus brought Revelation of what God is really like and how we are designed to live when not dominated by another kingdom. If there is any area of your life that is not dominated by kingdom principles of the *"way, the truth, and the life,"* then you are not experiencing the fullness of kingdom living as your divine designer has intended.

For the kingdom of God is not meat and drink; but righteousness, and peace, and joy in the Holy Ghost. Romans 14:17

The kingdom of God is not about food and drink, or wearing the right hairstyles, the right clothes, etc. It's not about having the right doctrine on every possible subject in the Bible.

At one point in my ministry I was a member of a certain denomination. There came a point when I realized that it was more about belief structures according to the group I was in than *"righteousness, and peace and joy in the Holy Ghost."* I realized that I had to always be in agreement of opinion on the basis of whatever the denomination said was right. They adopted the philosophy of, *"If we want your opinion, we will give it to you!"* It became nothing more than the law of the scribes and Pharisees under the label Christian. I discovered a large part of the denominational mission was to cause people to leave the current group they were in to join ours. After all we were the ones that were pure in doctrine, the container of all "truth."

I am convinced the body of Christ will never agree on all

of the different issues. Not understanding the real meaning of the gospel of the Kingdom has caused our churches to be inhabited by those who would teach and preach on just about every subject except the kingdom of God. It is amazing to me that all the different groups use the same Bible and yet somehow manage to create divisions over the meaning of Scripture, and the constant striving to be the only group that is pure. Is it any wonder why most denominations are irrelevant today? Could it be because the preaching of the gospel of the Kingdom is missing, resulting in massive confusion about the real meaning of our mission and mandate?

Without animosity in my heart I decided it was time to follow the leadership of the Holy Ghost and not the dictates of others. So I left, and never looked back.

As one old-time preacher used to say, *"There are no theological examinations to be passed at the gates of heaven!"* Real Kingdom living is not about everyone agreeing, but realizing we are in a family. And, the last time I looked families never agree on everything all the time. It's not about a religion where everyone marches in lockstep, but about a family that loves one another even in times of disagreement. A family does not exist because they agree, they exist because they have the same DNA of their father!

It's Time To Get Real

The original mandate to the first Adam was to have

dominion over the earth. The dominion given to Adam and Eve included both the visible material and the invisible spiritual realm. God blessed them and said to: *be fruitful; multiply; replenish the earth; subdue the earth and rule over every living thing.*

And God blessed them, and God said unto them, Be fruitful, and multiply, and replenish the earth, and subdue it: and have dominion over the fish of the sea, and over the fowl of the air, and over every living thing that moveth upon the earth. Genesis 1:28

God's purpose in creation was to have a family with royal blood made in His image according to his likeness. Carrying the DNA of the King was beyond description. There came a point when this perfect creation called Adam was put to the test. Adam and Eve made a choice. They chose disobedience. It was high treason. In their failure to obey God (which was their sin) they surrendered authority to Satan (See Genesis 3). They didn't fall from Heaven. They lost the right of dominion, and something had to be done to take it back.

Why did Jesus become the "last" Adam? To qualify as the last Adam (not second Adam) he had to become a man in order to redeem and restore everything the first Adam gave away. Through his obedience to the Father He became the perfect sacrifice for sin, defeated death, and restored the kingdom of God for all men – Now, that is good news!

The people of God have been living under the veil of deception for centuries when it comes to understanding two things; who we are in Christ, and the real meaning and mission of the church.

If I were going to devise a plan to stop God's authority and government on the earth, I would not go after Him. I would go after the ones to whom He has entrusted the "rights, privileges, and responsibilities" to carry out His mandate on the earth. Jesus came to take back authority, not His but ours. He came to restore fellowship with the Father, not His but ours. In order to do that he became a man:

But made himself of no reputation, and took upon him the form of a servant, and was made in the likeness of men: Philippians 2:7

And so it is written, the first man Adam was made a living soul; the LAST ADAM (Jesus) was made a quickening spirit. Howbeit that was not first which is spiritual, but that which is natural; and afterward that which is spiritual. The first man is of the earth, earthy; the second man is the Lord from heaven. 1 Corinthians 15:45-47

You can see in the ministry of Jesus the transfer of authority was already taking place. There were many in his day (and in our day) who think Jesus was some kind, gentle, sweet little teacher who walked around telling everybody just to get along. Jesus, meek and mild not wanting to cause trouble for anyone.

If you think that, it might be helpful to "read the red print" and see:

- He established authority over the law of nature by walking on water. Matthew 14:25
- He exercised control over the forces of nature, altering weather patterns. Mark 4:39
- He demonstrated authority over the laws of physics by: multiplying food; turning water into wine; translating His body from one place to another; and destroying trees simply by speaking to them. Matthew 15:36; John 2:9; 6:21; Mark 11:13 – 14.
- He had dominion over disease, healing multitudes. Acts 10:38
- He displayed power over the last enemy of man, death, by bringing ☐dead people back to life. John 11:43

Although everyone around him missed what he was doing, the enemy certainly understood Jesus was taking back authority. Having understood that, what would Satan do? **Cause the greatest identity crisis in the history of man!**

THE MEANING OF THE CHURCH

And I say also unto thee, that thou art Peter, and upon this rock I will build my church; and the gates of hell shall not prevail against it. And I will give unto thee the keys of the kingdom of heaven: and whatsoever thou shalt bind on earth shall be bound in heaven: and whatsoever thou shalt loose on earth shall be loosed in heaven. Matthew 16:18-19

You may be wondering, *"Brother Caldwell, what do those verses really mean, and does it apply to us today?"* I am so glad you asked.

I'm sure you've noticed already that I love to take apart a verse or two to discover its real meaning?

Let's break it down and see what Jesus was really saying to Peter:

And I say also unto thee, that thou art Peter, and upon this rock I will build my church;

If you go back and read the preceding verses you will see that Jesus asked a question; *"Whom do men say that I the Son of man am?"* While the other disciples gave different responses it was Simon Peter who, *"answered and said, Thou art the Christ, the Son of the living God."*

Good answer Peter! Jesus accepted his confession and used it to build a new revelation.

"That thou art Peter, (the Greek word "petros" means a "stone") *and upon this rock* (the Greek word "petra" means a large rock) *I will build my church;"*

In John 1:42 Jesus gave Simon the new name of Peter which means "a stone." The Aramaic form of Cephas, also means "a stone." Every individual who confesses Jesus as the son of God is called a "living stone" (1 Peter 2:5).

It is Jesus Christ who is the foundation rock on which the church is built! It is not Peter, much to the dismay of an entire denomination. There is no way God would build his church on a fallible man like Peter who one minute confessed Christ and the next minute he spewed curse words and denied he ever met him. Needless to say Peter had his problems, and if you still don't believe me go to Galatians 2 and read about Paul's rebuke of Peter.

"I will build my church"

When you think of the word "church" what comes to mind? After all, in most cities there is one on every corner. Today, we have churches of just about every conceivable flavor. We have churches that look like dressed up funeral parlors to Six Flags over Jesus. From funeral songs to the latest hip-hop entertainment from Hollywood, you name it we have it!

For centuries we have been fooled, hoodwinked, and deceived into believing the mission of the church was nothing more than to be a sanctified civic organization. Tragically the only difference between a local church on the corner, and the Moose club, (You can include your favorite civic organization here), is the church members don't have to wear Moose hats on Sunday morning. I have nothing against civic organizations, they do a lot of good, but that is not what Jesus gave his life for! (See Ephesians 5).

46

Like any good civic organization the church has its own secret language, dues (tithes), rules to follow, and restricted membership. By restricted I mean to be a member of the average church you need to dress like, think like, and act like everyone else. And, God forbid should you ever color outside of the lines. The last thing you want to do is declare, *"I have a revelation from God."* Believe me, if you do you can expect a visit from the "rules committee," who will determine if you can stay a member in good standing.

We have somehow been convinced the mission of the church is to meet on Sunday morning, sing a few choruses, take an offering, and give a Bible lesson. Nothing wrong with any of that, but there may be a little more to our mandate than just showing up once a week and going through the motions of "church."

It might be a good idea to ask the founder what he thinks about it.

When Jesus said **"I will build my church,"** He was making a declaration:

- I am the head of the church – you are not.
- Everything must flow from the head down, not the bottom up.
- I paid for the right of ownership – you didn't.

This is the first time the word *"church"* is used in the New Testament. The Greek word is *"ekklesia."* The literal meaning is *"a called out assembly."* The word is used 114 times in the New Testament.

When Jesus used the word *"church"* the disciples had no problem understanding what He was talking about. The reason we are confused today about the church is in large part due to our "western way" of thinking that the church is nothing more than a group of people who meet once a week, and have no relevant impact on society.

- To the Greeks the *"ekklesia"* was an assembly of people set apart to govern ☐the affairs of the state or nation, much like a Parliament or Congress.
- To the Romans the *"ekklesia"* was a group of people sent into a conquered region to alter the culture until it became a "Rome away from Rome." The Romans knew this was the best way to control the Empire. They infiltrated government, language, social structure until the people talked, thought, and acted like Romans.

The people of God are God's representatives on the earth. We are to colonize. A colony is *"a company of people transplanted from their mother country to a remote province or country. The colony remains subject to the jurisdiction of the parent state; as, the British colonies in America."*

☐*"For our conversation (<u>citizenship</u>) is in heaven; from whence ☐also we look for the Saviour, the Lord Jesus Christ:" Philippians 3:20*

48

God's intent was to plant a colony of His citizens on the earth to make His manifold wisdom known to the rulers and authorities in the heavenly realms!

How do I know?

Paul said so*: " Unto me, who am less than the least of all saints, is this grace given, that I should preach among the Gentiles the unsearchable riches of Christ; And to make all men see what is the fellowship of the mystery, which from the beginning of the world hath been hid in God, who created all things by Jesus Christ: To the intent that now unto the principalities and powers in heavenly places might be known by the church the manifold wisdom of God, According to the eternal purpose which he purposed in Christ Jesus our Lord: Ephesians 3:8-11*

The bottom line is colonization was and is God's intent and system to extend Heaven's influence on the earth.

THE MISSION OF THE CHURCH

A mission statement is simply a one sentence, clear, concise statement that describes who you are; what you do; for whom and where. That's it, nothing more nothing less.

The ministry statement for Randy Caldwell ministries is: *"Revealing the true freedom that comes from living in the kingdom of God."*

Because I travel so much I'm able to interact with lots of

people in many different churches. I see all kinds of expressions of what we would call "church." I go to some churches whose main focus of expression is praise and worship. While others express themselves in teaching and training. Yet others focus on entertainment. I'm not saying those things are necessarily wrong, but if you want to find out the mission statement of the church it might be good again to go and ask the founder.

The head of the church gave a clear concise mission statement:

And Jesus came and spake unto them, saying, All power is given unto me in heaven and in earth. Go ye therefore, and teach all nations, baptizing them in the name of the Father, and of the Son, and of the Holy Ghost: Teaching them to observe all things whatsoever I have commanded you: and, lo, I am with you always, even unto the end of the world. Amen. Matthew 28:18-20

The basis of the Lord's "marching orders" is His authority. *"All authority hath been given me,"* declared the risen Lord. The Greek term *"exousia"* is translated *"authority."* It literally means "the right to use power."

Throughout his gospel Matthew stresses the authority of Jesus Christ. Jesus demonstrated His authority In His:

- Teaching (7:29).
- Healing (8:1-13).
- Forgiving sins (9:6).
- Authority over Satan (10:1).

The Greek verb translated *"go"* means *"as you are going."* The direct command of the mission of the church is to "make disciples." To fully understand our mission statement we need to heed His command of*: "While you are going, make disciples of all nations."* No matter what else we do, if we don't do that, we are not representing Him on the earth!

The most popular name for the early believers was "disciple." Being a disciple is more than just a convert to Christianity or a good church member. A disciple is too busy learning to get involved with petty church politics. The disciple is too busy asking "what's the next assignment" instead of "have you heard the latest rumor." A disciple is too busy "taking up his cross and dying to self" instead of trying to put someone else on the cross and crucifying them with their tongue!

The great deception is being played out on a relational level. As I have said before we have missed it by light years. We have not understood who we are *(disciple – a learner, a pupil of Christ)* or what our authority is. Instead of colonizing the planet, and spreading the influence of the kingdom of God we have become like a policeman who has graduated from the academy but can't make an arrest. Authority has been given to us, not power. God has all power necessary to back up anything He releases in the atmosphere. Please hear me when I tell you God will not release any of His power until the race of people, the humans He gave authority to opens up their mouth and begins to call those things that are not as though they were! The identity crisis is eliminated once you know who you are and who you belong to.

We are to declare the Gospel of the Kingdom. It is the only message of the Church that will transform individual lives, and in turn transform the culture in which we live. I am fed up with us missing the message of the gospel. The message of the gospel is not just "salvation for your soul." The message of the gospel is the Kingdom, and in the Kingdom is wrapped up everything needed for the whole man. There is salvation, healing, peace of mind, and everything you need. It is all wrapped up in the gospel of the kingdom! There is a world of lost and dying men waiting to hear the "Good News" of the Gospel of the Kingdom!

In the next chapter I want to show you that we are not slaves, subjects or soldiers. We are *sons, citizens, and ambassadors* of the King of Kings and Lord of Lords! As such, we have a Royal mandate to represent Him on the planet. You have royal blood flowing through your veins, and it's time to start acting like it!

Whatever you do, don't get off the bus. I am taking you somewhere!

Chapter 4

SONS, CITIZENS, AMBASSADORS

But when the fulness of the time was come, God sent forth his Son, made of a woman, made under the law, to redeem them that were under the law, that we might receive the adoption <u>of sons</u>. Galatians 4:4-5

Now therefore ye are no more strangers and foreigners, but <u>fellowcitizens</u> with the saints, and of the household of God; Ephesians 2:19

Now then we are <u>ambassadors for Christ</u>, as though God did beseech you by us: we pray you in Christ's stead, be ye reconciled to God. 2 Corinthians 5:20

Several years ago I had a friend, Brother Gary, who brought to my attention how much Jesus actually spoke about the Kingdom of God. Since that day God has poured revelation into my spirit about the importance of the message of the Kingdom. One aspect of the revelation has to do with who we really are. Is it possible that we are more than just "Sunday morning saints?" Is it possible that we have misunderstood what it means to be a child of God?

Before we get to that, let me remind you it was God's intent to colonize the earth with His citizens. Because of Adam and Eve's rebellion the original concept of kingdom and dominion was temporarily lost. Adam and Eve may have been taken by surprise by the sudden turn of events, but God was not. Immediately after their rebellion God put into motion His plan of restoration.

You might be thinking; *"Well brother Caldwell, it sure looks like the devil got one over on God. After all, he caused God's prized possession to rebel against Him!"*

You know, sometimes I think we give the devil way too much credit. Before you get too excited about Adam and Eve getting kicked out of the garden I need to remind you what God said to the devil:

And I will put enmity between thee and the woman, and between thy seed and her seed; it shall bruise thy head, and thou shalt bruise his heel. Genesis 3:15

When God addressed the devil He did so with kingdom implications. He referred to the woman's *"seed"* as singular, referring to one specific offspring that would crush the Devil's head. If you follow the *"seed"* thread throughout Scripture it becomes clear that God had a plan from the very beginning.

In Genesis 12 (and thereafter) the Messiah is to be the seed of Abraham, *"for in thy seed, as of one, shall all the families of the earth be blessed."* In Genesis 49 Jacob turned to his fourth son Judah and said, *"The scepter shall not depart from Judah, nor a lawgiver from between his feet, until Shiloh come; and unto him shall be the gathering of the people be."* The Messiah, the Savior shall be born of the tribe of Judah. In 2 Samuel 7 we learn that God promised to David a son who shall sit upon his throne and reign for ever and ever... *"Of the increase of his government and peace there shall be no end, upon the throne of David, and upon his kingdom, to order it, and to establish it with judgment and with justice from henceforth even for ever. The zeal of the Lord of hosts will perform this.* (Isaiah 9:7) Centuries later the "seed" would appear as the man Jesus Christ of Nazareth.

When Jesus stepped into history His message was not a message of religion, but of the Kingdom of God (Matthew 4:17). He announced it was time to *"repent,"* for the *"kingdom has shown back up on the earth."* It was time to change your way of thinking about everything you have heard up until now! When Jesus stepped on the scene He was declaring what was previously unseen was now on the scene. In other words Jesus declared, *"I have brought the kingdom with me!"*

God's intention is to colonize the earth and extend His influence through His sons and daughters, citizens, and ambassadors; not slaves, subjects, or employees.

Let me say it again – Jesus did not come to the earth to establish religion, or even Christianity. He came to take back authority and dominion that was lost in the garden!

As a matter of fact He never called anyone a Christian. Not one time in the word of God does God label us as Christians. The phrase "Christians" (plural) is mentioned one time in the Bible. And, the term "Christian" is in only two verses of Scripture (See Acts 11:26; 26:28; 1 Peter 4:16). Most Bible scholars agree the first use of the term "Christians" was spoken by a bunch of pagans, who were idol worshipers. These pagans had encountered a group of people that had a relationship with

God, and quite frankly they did not know what to do with them. I have no problem with the term Christian. I understand what we are talking about when we use it. I just wanted to remind you it was not a compliment in the first century!

WE ARE SONS AND DAUGHTERS – NOT SERVANTS AND SLAVES

Religion produces servants, and a poverty mentality produces slaves. We are neither. I'm sure there are those who think I might be wrong. Before you make that judgment call understand it is helpful to know the context when things are said. I know Jesus said a servant heart is the key to greatness in the kingdom of God (see Matthew 20:26 – 27). He also said that He Himself came to serve rather than be served (see Matthew 20:28). Every bit of that is true. However, there may be a little bit more for you and I to understand.

A son or a daughter sees servanthood as a privilege and a pleasure, not an obligation. The spirit of religion will produce servanthood when it sees it can gain a sense of false humility which in turn produces a false sense of pride. Sons and daughters serve willingly because of who they are, not because they "have to." An attitude of gratitude will produce a servant's heart. Religion will serve only for what it can get out of the deal. Big difference don't you think?

You know one of the things I love to do is to break down Scripture and dig out golden nuggets. No better explanation of who we are as sons and daughters can be found than what the apostle Paul stated in Galatians 4.

"But, when the fullness of time was come, God sent forth his Son, made of a woman, made under the law, to redeem them that were under the law, that we might receive the adoption of sons. And because ye are sons, God hath sent forth the Spirit of his Son into your hearts, crying Abba Father. Wherefore, thou art no more a servant, but a son; and if a son, then an heir of God through Christ." Galatians 4:4 – 7

Two statements jump off the page:

"when the fullness of time was come" literally means*; "when the full number of days had arrived, when full preparation was made."* It was at the end of preparation *"God sent forth his son, made of a woman."* The Lord is never in a hurry. He moves, and He acts based on "timing" not time. The fullness of time is not based on the hands of a clock, but has everything to do with "times and seasons."

There are times when eons and eons pass before God's purposes are fulfilled. There was the "exact time" known only to God, chosen by Him, when Christ would be born. Likewise, there was an exact time when Christ would die, be buried and rise from the dead. There was an exact time when the Lord would ascend into heaven. And, there is an exact time known only to God when he shall return.

When Jesus was born the time was right religiously, culturally, and politically. His birth was not an accident. All preparations were complete for the King of Heaven to send His son to restore

His kingdom on the earth!

"to redeem them that were under the law, that we might receive the adoption of sons."

Among the blessings of the Christian experience is "adoption" (see Ephesians 1:5). The Greek word for adoption is *"huiothesia."* Paul used the word several times in his writing. It literally means *"the placing of a son,"* or putting him in the family. Paul is using legal language. He is referring to the fact we have legal rights and privileges based on our relationship to our heavenly Father. Jesus did not pay the ultimate price in his own blood to enlist servants and slaves. No, a thousand times NO! He paid the price to restore the King's sons and daughters to rulership as heirs of His Kingdom!

When you understand the biblical meaning of adoption it will eliminate for all time the idea of the universalism. There is no such thing in the Bible! While it's true God is the creator of all mankind there is no such thing as a universal brotherhood of man. Just as birth was required for you to enter your natural family, so is a spiritual birth required to enter the kingdom of God (see John 3; 1 Peter 1:22 – 25).You do not enter God's family through adoption – it is through regeneration. (*Later on we will talk in depth about the conversation between Jesus and Nicodemus. It's the only time Jesus talked about being born from above.*) But, for now you have to understand the only way to enter the kingdom is through the *new birth.*

Adoption has to do with our standing in the family of

God. When the new birth takes place our condition is a "spiritual baby" who needs to grow (see 1 Peter 2:2 – 3). It is not possible for a baby to legally use his inheritance. The little baby may have an inheritance on paper, but it does not become his to enjoy until he reaches legal age.

Adoption is the act of God by which He gives His "born ones" adult standing in the family. Our position as an adult son gives us immediate claim on our inheritance. We can enjoy our spiritual riches now! Our position as adult sons and daughters of the King means we don't have to wait until we are old chronologically to claim all the wealth of the kingdom.

As a child of the King we have "receive the full rights of sons and daughters."

- A son/daughter has the same nature (DNA) as the father – the slave does not.
- A son/daughter has intimate access to their father – the slave has a master who is unmoved, and unemotionally involved.
- A son/daughter is rich – the slave is poor.
- A son/daughter has a future – the slave is hopeless.
- A son/daughter obeys out of love – the slave obeys out of fear.

WE ARE CITIZENS – NOT SOLDIERS!

Citizenship carries great privileges. If you don't believe

me then why are thousands of people willing to break the law and risk their lives to enter this country? With all of her flaws, problems, and challenges, America is still the greatest nation on earth. People outside of this country look at the privileges we enjoy as citizens and know these privileges are not obtained easily. In spite of the danger they still cross our borders for the hope of obtaining the privileges and rights of a citizen.

When I talk about citizens of the kingdom of God I am not talking about religion. The kingdom of God is a government with the country. Jesus Christ is Its King, and the born again are its citizens.

As born again the citizens of the kingdom we need to understand that citizenship begins immediately. We do not have to wait until we die to enjoy the privileges of citizenship. The spirit of religion will tell you just the opposite. I've said it before, and I will say it again – GOD HATES RELIGION! It stinks to high heaven.

Religion wants to control every area of your life, past, present and future. The spirit of religion, the spirit of antichrist, will try to control your past by making you feel guilty over everything you have ever done. It will try to control your present with a "Gotcha God" who is portrayed as nothing more than a policeman with a club. It will try to control your future with doubt and fear.

The spirit of religion will tell you that you can never enjoy the privileges of Kingdom citizenship now. It wants you to believe it's for some future time. You can experience healing, just not now. You can know joy, just not now. You can operate in kingdom economics and abundance, just not now. That my friend is a lie!

1. Because we are citizens of the kingdom of God we should act like it.

"For our citizenship is in heaven, from which also we look for the Savior, the Lord Jesus Christ." Philippians 3:20

The child of God enjoys dual citizenship – on earth and in heaven. The Greek word translated *"conversation" or "citizenship"* is the word from which we get the English word *"politics."* The literal meaning has to do with the behavior or actions of a citizen of a nation.

The apostle Paul was writing to the church at Philippi. They had no trouble understanding the importance of citizenship. Philippi was a conquered territory, a colony, which meant that even though it was many miles away it was still considered a part of the "kingdom "of Rome. The citizens of Philippi were not governed by Greek law, but

Roman law. If you were a Roman citizen, it did not matter how far you traveled from the central government, you still enjoyed all the rights and privileges of a Roman citizen.

2. Because we are citizens of the kingdom of God we don't have to fight our own battles.

Paul was a Roman citizen and he used that right for

protection on several occasions...*"But Paul said unto them, They have beaten us openly uncondemned, being Romans, and have cast us into prison; and now do they thrust us out privily? nay verily; but let them come themselves and fetch us out. And the serjeants told these words unto the magistrates: and they feared, when they heard that they were Romans. (Acts 16:37 – 38).* Paul knew he did not have to fight his own battles, all he had to do was declare his citizenship. Your personal safety, as well as your personal freedom, was guaranteed by the full force of the most powerful nation on earth.

I can still remember the little song we used to sing when I was a kid, *"I'm in the Lord's army."* As I grew older the songs changed, but the meaning was still the same. We sang songs like *"Onward Christian soldiers – marching off to war."* That sounds real spiritual doesn't? Only one thing wrong with it – it is just flat out wrong! Not one time does the Bible call believers the Army of God. The phrase "armies of the living God" is only found two times in the Bible (See 1 Samuel 17).

We are not the Army of God, we are citizens of the kingdom of God. Kingdoms have citizens and citizens are not soldiers. Citizens do not fight. The Army fights, and defends its citizens. The question that has to be answered is; *"Who are the soldiers in the Army of the kingdom of heaven?"* if it is not its citizens then who? I'm glad you asked.

Jesus' encounter with Pilate gives us some insight:

When Jesus was arrested and brought before Pilate he

never said a word. I believe it was because Jesus knew this process, this mock trial had to be played out. He knew for the plan of salvation, and program of the Kingdom to work He was going to pay the ultimate price – death on the cross. Therefore, there was no need to say anything. (See John 18).

But, the atmosphere shifts when Pilate begins to talk about rulership, power and authority. Jesus knew that Pilate had no idea what he was talking about so He opened up and corrected him. When Pilate asked Jesus *"Are you a king?"* Jesus simply responded *"What do you say Pilate?* Then Pilate wanted to know if you are a king why don't your servants come and rescue you?

Now, things are about to get interesting.

"Jesus answered, My kingdom is not of this world; if my kingdom were of this world, then would my servants fight, that I should not be delivered to the Jews; but now is my kingdom not from here." John 18:36

When Pilate heard the answer of Jesus he's beginning to get worried and says *"Are you a king then?"* Jesus answered, *"Thou say just that I am a king. To this end was I born, and for this cause came I into the world, that I should bear witness unto the truth. Everyone that is of the truth heareth my voice." John 18:37*

"When Pilate, therefore, heard that saying, he was the more afraid; And when again into the judgment hall and saith unto Jesus, From where art thou? But Jesus gave him no answer. Then saith Pilate unto him, Speakest thou not unto

me? Knowest thou not that I have power to crucify thee, and have power to release thee? Jesus answered, thou couldest have no power at all against me, except it were given thee from above; therefore, he that delivered me unto thee hath the greater sin." John 19:8-11

In the Gospel of Matthew the conversation is expanded. Jesus said you want to talk about power? Let's talk... *"Thinkest thou that I cannot now pray to my Father, and he shall presently give me more than 12 legions of angels? (Matthew 26:53)*.

Pilate said, *"if you are a king, where's your army at?"* Jesus said, *"My kingdom is not of this world if it was my servants would fight for me."* Jesus let Pilate know that he had 12 legions of angels at his disposal. They were more than ready, willing, and able to come to his rescue. *"Don't you understand Pilate I can pray and stop all of this if I need it stopped?"*

A Legion is six thousand. Jesus said I have 12 legions or a total of 72,000 of my warriors on standby.

The prophet Isaiah tells us that one angel killed 185,000 Assyrians in one night! (Isaiah 37:36). If one Angel can kill 185,000, then one Legion of 6000 angels could kill 1 billion, 110 million – right? But, it gets worse. Jesus said He could bring 72,000 of his warriors. Now if you multiply it out 72,000 Angels could wipe out 13 billion, 320 million people, which is more than double the current world population! These are some bad dudes, and believe me Pilate you don't want to mess with them.

Jesus made it very clear to Pilate, "*You are one lucky guy. You are not taking my life, I am laying it down. If my kingdom was of this world I could wipe out the entire planet.*" Wiping out the planet was not the plan. I willingly give my life because I have come with the government upon my shoulders (Isaiah 9:6-7), to be the Prince of Peace and to reestablish Kingdom rights back to its citizens.

The word "servants" in the Greek is "huperestes." It literally means *"underrowing, an officer, and attendant of a magistrate, the attendant of the King or the soldiers of the King."* The servants, or soldiers that Jesus referred to are not his disciples, but angels!

So, I repeat –Kingdoms have citizens and citizens are not soldiers. Citizens do not fight. The Army fights, and defends its citizens. The Army serves its citizens.

As a citizen you and I have the ability in our country to call on law enforcement when a problem arises. As a citizen you have the authority to pick up the phone, make one call and the "army" shows up at your house. The army may be called the city police, the County Sheriff, but the results are the same. They are there to protect and defend your rights as a citizen.

What most Christians do instead of walking in the authority of kingdom citizens is trying to fight the forces of evil by themselves. You and I do not have the power to fight, but we do have the authority to release those that know how to fight! You have a direct line into heaven – it's called prayer! You can pick up the prayer line and dispatch an army of angels at any given moment. You can fire a spiritual ICBM missile from any space as small as your bed, or closet, and hit a target halfway around the world – **HALLELUJAH!**

You might be thinking to yourself – *"Hold on Brother Caldwell what about Paul encouraging us to put on the whole armor of God in Ephesians 6:10?*

Time and space won't allow me to give you all the details. But, I will tell you we are to put on the whole armor of God for the purposes of standing, not attacking. God says in His kingdom I don't want you getting hit by a stray bullet. I don't want you damaged by shrapnel. Therefore, put on the whole armor of God that you may be able to withstand the evil day and having done all **STAND!** In other words, just stand real still because the Army is on its way.

I will tell you my friend, as a citizen of the kingdom you are protected. You have God's promise that His army, (Angels) are ready and willing to fight on your behalf. They have been given charge to help you, therefore you have nothing to worry about (Psalm 78:49; 91:7; 103:19 – 22; Hebrews 1:14).

So stop trying to fight battles God never intended for you to fight. It could be the reason you continue to get your brains beat out. It's time to stop trying to be something that God never intended for you to be.

Enjoy your citizenship – you are covered!

God does not want subjects. Why? Subjects are under oppressive rule of a dictator. Ambassadors walk, talk, and live with authority given them by their government.

Now then we are <u>ambassadors for Christ</u>, as though God did beseech you by us: we pray you in Christ's stead, be ye reconciled to God. 2 Corinthians 5:20

When Paul called us ambassadors for Christ you have to understand what an ambassador is. Ambassadors are servants of their government in a foreign land. An ambassador is an envoy or minister of a state sent on a mission by one sovereign or state to another. An ambassador is a spokesperson or representative of one state with authority to speak to the authorities of another state.

Ambassadors are not free to set their own policies or develop their own message. In the same way, we are called to live under the authority of Jesus Christ and the authority of the Scriptures. We are called not to do our will, but Christ's. We represent the Kingdom of God in a foreign and an alien world. We are citizens of two communities–the community of God and the community in which we live.

In my lifetime I have been blessed to travel this planet. I have been on six out of seven continents. The only one I have missed is Antarctica, which by the way was by choice not by accident. When I am in a country that is friendly to America I make it a point to visit its capital, and make my way to the American Embassy.

I can still remember the last time I visited Nairobi Kenya. I found something utterly amazing. There is a particular Valley that has over 1 million people living in total abject poverty. Their houses are made out of mud and cow manure. The back wall of one house is the wall of his neighbor's house. The top of the house has nothing more than a piece of tin laid on top. The streets are filthy. Disease is rampant. But, if you turn around from that Valley and look down the street there is an American embassy that has the most immaculate manicured lawn you will ever see. It is literally the most beautiful building in town. It is protected by some of the biggest Marines this country can produce. I mean these are some bad looking dudes. Not only do they have weapons at the ready, they don't seem to have much of a sense of humor when it comes to someone wanting to come through the gates without proper identification.

You may be thinking, *"Oh, Brother Randy that's just awful to show wealth like that in such an impoverished nation."* My answer to you would be – *no it is not.* It is what ambassadors do. You see my friend no matter what kind of shape the economy is in if you are an ambassador of another nation you're economic standard is determined by where you are from, not where you are living. An ambassador does not have to depend on the local economy to meet his needs.

Jesus came to set up the kingdom of heaven so that you

and I could enjoy all of the privileges of an ambassador. That is why if Wall Street has a problem you don't have to worry about it. If the housing market crumbles, and the economy goes down the drain you are still protected. You live by the economic standards of another world, and in that world there is a street of gold, walls of Jasper, and gates of Pearl.

"To wit, that God was in Christ, reconciling the world unto himself, not imputing their trespasses unto them; and hath committed unto us the word of reconciliation." 2 Corinthians 5:19

The governing body of heaven has now given us the official position. As ambassadors we have been given the authority to speak on its behalf. We have been entrusted with the message of reconciliation. The apostle Paul declared in 1 Thessalonians 2:4 – *"But as we were allowed of God to be put in trust with the gospel, even so we speak; not as pleasing men, but God, which trieth our hearts."*

In the Roman Empire, there were two kinds of provinces: senatorial provinces and imperial provinces. The senatorial provinces were those who submitted to Rome and were considered no threat. They were peaceful and obeyed Roman law. But, the imperial provinces were not peaceful nor were they inclined to obey. They were dangerous to the Roman way of life. They would undermine the law and rebel at the drop of a hat. The government of Rome determined to send ambassadors to the imperial provinces to make sure that rebellion would not break out.

As Christians we know what it means to be reconciled to God. As ambassadors we now have the privilege of sharing the message of reconciliation with the world system that is in rebellion against God.

Jesus said that we are *"in"* the world, but not *"of"* the world. But he also stated that He is sending us *"into"* the world (See John 17). We are sent into the world that is in rebellion against God. As far as the government of Heaven is concerned the world is an "imperial providence." As ambassadors of Christ we have the message of reconciliation. It is the official position of Heaven that "peace" not "war" has been declared.

Wherefore remember, that ye being in time past Gentiles in the flesh, who are called Uncircumcision by that which is called the Circumcision in the flesh made by hands; That at that time ye were without Christ, being aliens from the commonwealth of Israel, and strangers from the covenants of promise, having no hope, and without God in the world: But now in Christ Jesus ye who sometimes were far off are made nigh by the blood of Christ.

For he is our peace, who hath made both one, and hath broken down the middle wall of partition between us; Having abolished in his flesh the enmity, even the law of commandments contained in ordinances; for to make in himself of twain one new man, so making peace; And that he might reconcile both unto God in one body by the cross, having slain the enmity thereby: And came and preached peace to you which were afar off, and to them that were nigh. For through him we both have access by one Spirit unto the Father.

Now therefore ye are no more strangers and foreigners, but fellowcitizens with the saints, and of the household of God; Ephesians 2:11-19

I think it's about time that we stop acting like Sunday morning saints, and scared little children that run from our own shadow.

It's time to start acting like:

- Sons and daughters who enjoy intimate fellowship with our heavenly Father.
- Citizens who have rights and privileges of the kingdom of God.
- Ambassadors who carry this treasure in earthen vessels, and have the privilege of speaking on behalf of our King!

Chapter 5

CONFLICT IN THE CORNFIELD

At that time Jesus went on the sabbath day through the corn; and his disciples were an hungred, and began to pluck the ears of corn and to eat. But when the Pharisees saw it, they said unto him, Behold, thy disciples do that which is not lawful to do upon the sabbath day. Matthew 12:1-2

Before we look at the encounter between Jesus and the Pharisees keep in mind that Matthew 12 is simply a part of a 24 hour day that began in Matthew 11. I remind people all the time that the Bible was not written in chapter and verse. If we are not careful we will read the Scriptures, and certain events as if they were isolated and not connected. Failure to connect will lead to confusion.

CONTEXT IS IMPORTANT

Matthew 12:1 says, "At That Time." Now, if you are like I am, when you read the first three words of Matthew 12 you have to take pause and ask yourself a question: *"At what time is Matthew talking about?"* To find out the time Matthew is referring to you have to go back to Matthew chapter 11 and read in context.

At about eight or eight thirty in the morning Jesus spoke about John the Baptist. Jesus declared in *Matthew 11:7-11: "And as they departed, Jesus began to say unto the multitudes concerning John, What went ye out into the wilderness to see?*

A reed shaken with the wind? But what went ye out for to see? A man clothed in soft raiment? behold, they that wear soft clothing are in kings' houses. But what went ye out for to see? A prophet? yea, I say unto you, and more than a prophet. For this is he, of whom it is written, Behold, I send my messenger before thy face, which shall prepare thy way before thee. Verily I say unto you, Among them that are born of women there hath not risen a greater than John the Baptist: notwithstanding he that is least in the kingdom of heaven is greater than he.

Now, I'm am going to show you something that the Holy Spirit has revealed to me, and it's a heavy statement. Jesus just told the people *"that no greater prophet has been born of a woman than John the Baptist."* But, in the very next verse he said *"that the least in the kingdom is greater than John the Baptist!"* I don't know about you but when I hear a statement like that my mind has trouble comprehending the revelation. He was saying all that have been born up until that point including: Adam, Moses Abraham, Noah, all of the righteous kings, including King David, and certainly all of the prophets could not compare to the greatness of John the Baptist. Believe me that was just a short list, feel free to add more names.

Here is what I believe Jesus was saying: *"The least that is in the kingdom, that I am here to set up, is greater than John the Baptist." Wow!* Jesus declared that John the Baptist was "the transition man," who stood between law and grace. Jesus put John in a position that not even he stood in, that is a hinge

73

between two dispensations. I'm not saying that John was greater than Jesus, but as the forerunner John's message was, *"Repent, for the Kingdom of Heaven is at hand."* It's all about the Kingdom, always has been, always will be!

So, understanding the context is important. Matthew 11 is revelation of the kingdom, and now Matthew 12 is just a continuation of that revelation. Matthew is now going to use an event to illustrate not only the revelation of the kingdom, but how the religious spirit confronts it.

At that time Jesus went on the sabbath day through the corn; and his disciples were an hungred, and began to pluck the ears of corn and to eat. **But when the Pharisees (The religious crowd, <u>the religious spirited people that has caused more trouble in the church than any of the spirit</u>)** *saw it, they said unto him, Behold, thy disciples do that which is not lawful to do upon the sabbath day.* **But he said unto them, Have ye not read what David did, when he was an hungred, and they that were with him; How he entered into the house of God, and did eat the shewbread, which was not lawful for him to eat, neither for them which were with him, but only for the priests?*

Or have ye not read in the law, how that on the sabbath days the priests in the temple profane the sabbath, and are blameless? But I say unto you, That in this place is one greater than the temple. But if ye had known what this meaneth, I will have mercy, and not sacrifice, ye would not have condemned the guiltless. For the Son of man is Lord even of the sabbath

74

day. (Matthew 12:1-8).

I want you to picture the scene in your mind. Jesus and His disciples are walking through a field of grain on the Sabbath day. The disciples are hungry and decided to pluck some of the grain and eat it. The Pharisees saw what the disciples did, and began to confront Jesus with criticism for allowing his disciples to "break the Sabbath law." It seems to me the Pharisees made it their life mission to find Jesus doing something wrong. Is it just me, or have you noticed that on more than one occasion the Pharisees would "pop-up" out of nowhere and point their fingers at Jesus to accuse him? Each time they tried to make a "citizen's arrest," Jesus refused to back down.

I have made many trips to Israel. I happen to know where Jesus fed the 5000 (not counting women and children) is the same place where the disciples plucked the corn. The nearest synagogue is approximately 5 miles from that spot. So the Pharisees, on the Sabbath, had to walk at least 5 miles to get to where Jesus was. It was against the law to walk more than 2 miles on the Sabbath. It's funny to me that the pharisaical control (the spirit of religion) was criticizing someone for what they thought was wrong, while at the same time overlooking the fact they had their own problems. In other words, they were breaking their own law. You will be stunned at the distance your enemy will travel just to tear you down and criticize you. No wonder Jesus called them hypocrites! (See Matthew 23).

This would not be the first or last time they accused Him

75

of violating Sabbath traditions. I will give them credit for one thing. They were relentless in trying to keep Jesus in their box of religious traditions. But, every time they tried to stop Him, he would color outside the lines! Jesus confronted the spirit of religion, not with opinion, but with cold hard facts.

HAVE YOU NOT READ?

Don't you love it when Jesus takes the Scripture and uses it as a sharp two edged sword! He did it when tempted by Satan, and now He uses the same sword when confronted by the Pharisees. He didn't argue with them, he simply throws it back in their face.

The Pharisees said what the disciples were doing was wrong. Were they right to make the accusation? No, absolutely not!

Jesus pulled out the sword and said **"have you not read?"** In other words, He pointed out something they should already know. Yes, *it was lawful to satisfy your hunger from your neighbor's field according to Deuteronomy 23:24 – 25.*

When thou comest into thy neighbour's vineyard, then thou mayest eat grapes thy fill at thine own pleasure; but thou shalt not put any in thy vessel. When thou comest into the standing corn of thy neighbour, then thou mayest pluck the ears with thine hand; but thou shalt not move a sickle unto thy neighbour's standing corn.

Of course the Pharisees knew that, but they added their own interpretations and traditions on top of the Scriptures. You see, that's what the spirit of religion will do! It will take the clear teaching of the word of God and twist it to fit its own interpretation and man-made tradition. If we are not careful we will fall into the same trap of making our own traditions, and preferences equal to the commandments of God. There is a big difference between traditions and traditionalism. There is an old saying that goes like this: *"Tradition is the living faith of those now dead. Traditionalism is the dead faith of those who are alive."*

Later on in Matthew 15 Jesus warned them again when he said –*"**Thus have ye made the commandment of God of none effect by your tradition."***

He refused to allow them to place burdens of traditionalism onto the shoulders of His followers. In Matthew 23:4 ***He said, "They tie up heavy loads and put them on men's shoulders, but they themselves are not willing to lift a finger to move them."***

One of the underlying root causes of "church wars" is when we substitute our personal preferences over the clear teaching of the Bible. You may not like the same type of music that I like. You may not read from the same Bible translation that I do. Does that make me right, and you wrong? I could mess with you right now (which is one of my favorite pastimes) and say, yes, my preferences are better than yours, so therefore I am right and you are wrong. Obviously, that is not true. Just because we prefer different things doesn't make either one of us right or wrong.

The spirit of religion is easy to identify. It never wants to talk about God's glory, or how wonderful it is that the Holy Spirit is moving in powerful ways in our church. No, it would rather gossip, back bite, and tear down anything it cannot control.

I like what one old-time preacher said – *if it's a matter of taste, or preference always show grace to the other person. If it's a matter of clear teaching in Scripture stand firm and don't back up!*

JESUS WAS NOT ABOUT TO BACK UP!

He is about to back them into a corner, and trap them with truth. When they offer criticism, He gives them a response for which they have no answer.

Watch what he does –He calls on 3 witnesses:

Witness 1...King David.

But he said unto them, have ye not read what David did, when he was an hungred, and they that were with him; How he entered into the house of God, and did eat the shewbread, which was not lawful for him to eat, neither for them which were with him, but only for the priests? (Matthew 12:3- 4)

David and his men ate consecrated bread that was to be eaten only by the priest (See 1 Samuel 21). Jesus, as the son of

David had every right to eat His Father's grain from the field. If David and his men were not condemned for breaking the law, surely Jesus could break man's traditions and be guiltless!

Witness 2…The Priests.

Or have ye not read in the law, how that on the sabbath days the priests in the temple profane the sabbath, and are blameless? (Matthew 12:5 – 6)

The priests were commanded to offer sacrifices on the Sabbath (See Numbers 28:9 – 10) and yet they were not guilty of breaking the law. God gave the law, and their service was in obedience to that very law. It is plain to see that man's teaching and traditions about the Sabbath were wrong. They were in direct contradiction to God's own law!

Witness 3…The Prophet

But I say unto you, That in this place is one greater than the temple. But if ye had known what this meaneth, I will have mercy, and not sacrifice, ye would not have condemned the guiltless. For the Son of man is Lord even of the sabbath day. (Matthew 12:7 – 8)

For the second time Jesus quotes Hosea 6:6 (See Matthew 9:13). While the Sabbath law was given as a sign of Israel's relationship to God (See Nehemiah 9:12 – 15; Exodus 20:9 – 11), it was also an act of mercy to give needed rest each week. The Sabbath law was not given to hang around the neck as a heavy stone, but rather it was given as an act of love.

When Jesus declared himself "Lord of the Sabbath," he was declaring equality with God. It was God who established the Sabbath (See Genesis 2:1 – 3). The Sabbath belonged to Him just as animals belong to their master. As Lord of the Sabbath Jesus could act with mercy what seemed best to him. Of course, the Pharisees were not about to stand up and applaud, quite the contrary. So, how did the Pharisees react to the declaration of Jesus? They plotted to kill Him – so much for religious tolerance!

NOW, FOR THE REST OF THE STORY

I believe there is more to this story than Jesus and his disciples stopping in a cornfield and having a quick lunch. There is a deeper spiritual meaning behind the physical confrontation between Jesus and the Pharisees.

I believe everything in the natural has spiritual meaning. There were 4 things about this confrontation that jumped off the page:

1. What were the disciples really hungry for?

While it's true they were hungry for physical food, *"and his disciples were an hungred, and began to pluck the ears of corn and to eat,"* I also believe they were hungry for spiritual revelation. When you look up the word "hungry" or "hungered" in Strong's concordance you will see *"that has neither past, present nor future time tied to it."* What the disciples were hungry for was to understand the revelation of the Kingdom Jesus just talked about in Matthew 11.

On the outside the Pharisees were upset because Jesus and the disciples were breaking the law according to their interpretation. But, behind the mask of religion was the fact that they were really upset because the disciples were hungry for revelation. They were losing control, and there was nothing they could do about it. The religious crowd will always be upset at those who are hungry for revelation about the Kingdom of God.

The spirit of religion (control) will tell you – *"Stay in the box, we have it all figured out. You don't have to study because we have studied for you. We have the answers, and you don't have to search any longer."*

Hear me well – God is not against the Assemblies of God, Baptists, Methodists, or any other denomination as long as it does not seek to control the lives of people. It is wonderful to form fellowships, but when that fellowship moves into control God will stand against it.

2. Corn is more than just food.

The word *corn* is mentioned 102 times in the Bible. It is in 92 verses and it is always symbolic of *revelation.*

"Verily, verily, I say unto you, Except a corn of wheat fall into the ground and die, it abideth alone: but if it die, it bringeth forth much fruit." John 12:24

In the Bible, corn is also used in connection with *wine and oil.*

81

Moses declared: *That I will give you the rain of your land in his due season, the first rain and the latter rain, that thou mayest gather in thy corn, and thy wine, and thine oil. Deuteronomy 11:14*

What a promise God has made to His people. But His promise came with a stipulation: "*And it shall come to pass, if ye shall hearken diligently unto My commandments which I command you this day, to love the Lord your God, and to serve Him with all your heart and with all your soul," Deuteronomy 11:13*

As God has promised, this gathering will only come to pass if we hearken diligently unto the Lord our God, and serve Him with all our heart and soul.

You may be thinking as I have, "*Why are we not seeing more revelation about the kingdom of God, and the power of God manifest in the church?*"

Haggai gives us insight: "*And I called for a drought upon the land, and upon the mountains, and upon the <u>corn</u>,* (REVELATION) *and upon the new wine,* (THE HOLY SPIRIT) *and upon the oil,* (DOUBLE PORTION ANOINTING) *and upon that which the ground bringeth forth, and upon men, and upon cattle, and upon all the labour of the hands." Haggai 1:11*

Haggai says God has brought a drought upon the land, a drought upon the corn, a drought upon the wine, a drought upon the oil, and a drought upon the ground and all the labor of men's' hands. Have you ever felt like you have been in a drought? If so, you are not alone. But I have good news, the drought is coming to an end! How do I know that? Because everywhere I go I see people who are thirsty for life-giving, life-changing revelation about the kingdom of God.

There is a day of refreshing coming when the new wine, the mature corn, and the double portion anointing of the Holy Spirit will be restored in God's people. **HALLELUJAH!**

"And it shall come to pass in that day that the mountains shall drop down new wine and the hills shall flow with milk, and all the rivers of Judah shall flow with waters, and a fountain shall come forth of the house of the Lord, and shall water the valley of Shittim." Joel 3:18

3. The Field is more than a patch of ground.

Corn is *revelation*, and the field is *opportunity.* There are four things you need to know about the field.

- *There are times when the field is closed, and the corn is not ripe.* That means there is no opportunity and no revelation. It is in these times where you have to simply walk by faith in the light that you already have.

- *There are times when the field is open but the corn is not ripe.* That means the opportunity may be there but there is no revelation. That's why some ministries only last for a brief time and disappear. What happened? They jumped too soon and ended up faking it. Nothing worse for a preacher to have nothing to say – and go ahead and say it anyway!

- *There are times when the field is closed, but the corn is ripe.* That means you have a word of revelation but no opportunity to share it. This is a frustrating time because you have a word but there are no open doors.
- *There are times when the field is open, and the corn is ripe.* I believe we are living in that time right now. People are hungry for revelation. God will always raise up the right man, at the right time, for the right season to stand against the kingdom of darkness!

4. Why David?

Jesus appealed to David, why? (Matthew 12:3-4). Obviously he was pointing to an episode in the life of David when he and his soldiers ate the showbread. David was "hungry," and if you fast-forward 1000 years you will notice the disciples had the same hunger. The hunger for "revelation" did not start when Jesus showed up.

When Jesus asked the Pharisees *"Have you not read what David did,"* I think he was talking about more than just eating the showbread. There is a deeper meaning. Just exactly what did David do?

Then came David to Nob to Ahimelech the priest: and Ahimelech was afraid at the meeting of David, and said unto him, Why art thou alone, and no man with thee? And David said unto Ahimelech the priest, The king hath commanded me

84

a business, and hath said unto me, Let no man know anything
of the business where about I send thee, and what I have
commanded thee: and I have appointed my servants to such
and such a place. Now therefore what is under thine hand?
Give me five loaves of bread in mine hand, or what there is
present. And the priest answered David, and said, there is no
common bread under mine hand, but there is hallowed bread;
if the young men have kept themselves at least from women.

And David answered the priest, and said unto him, Of a
truth women have been kept from us about these three days,
since I came out, and the vessels of the young men are holy,
and the bread is in a manner common, yea, though it were
sanctified this day in the vessel. So the priest gave him hallowed
bread: for there was no bread there but the shewbread, that was
taken from before the Lord, to put hot bread in the day when it
was taken away. Now a certain man of the servants of Saul was
there that day, detained before the Lord; and his name was
Doeg, an Edomite, the chiefest of the herdmen that belonged to
Saul. And David said unto Ahimelech, And is there not here
under thine hand spear or sword? for I have neither brought
my sword nor my weapons with me, because the king's business
required haste. And the priest said, The sword of Goliath the
Philistine, whom thou slewest in the valley of Elah, behold, it is
here wrapped in a cloth behind the ephod: if thou wilt take that,
take it: for there is no other save that here. And David said,
There is none like that; give it me. And David arose and fled

that day for fear of Saul, and went to Achish the king of Gath.
1 Samuel 21: 1-10

David came to Nob, and presented himself to Ahimelek the priest. It would be fair to say that Ahimelek was not thrilled.

Let me give you the Caldwell translation of the conversation between David and the priest:

Ahimelek*: "Dude, why are you here, and where are your men? David: "The King has sent me on a secret mission. That's all I can tell you."*

Ahimelek: *"If Saul finds out you are here he will kill both of us. You are putting me at risk. I hate to hurt your feelings, but I don't need to be seen with you!"*

David gives an answer that is on the surface confusing at best and lying at worst: ***"The king hath commanded me."*** Was David lying? Did the King Saul really appoint and commission him? David was on the Saul's "most wanted list," so how could David say the king had commanded him?

I don't believe David was lying at all. I'll tell you exactly what he was doing. The same thing Jesus did centuries later – he's speaking a parable. Jesus preached in parables. When the disciples asked him why He spoke that way He told them He talked in circles so the religious crowd would not understand what He was saying. David is doing exactly the same thing!

Earlier in 1 Samuel, Saul is rejected as King. David is anointed King in 1 Samuel 15-16. When David said to the priest,

"The King commanded me," what he was really saying is, *"I have commanded me."* David told the priest, "I have commanded myself, so therefore give me what I need, which in this case is something to eat – the showbread."

DAVID NEEDED A WEAPON

When David asked Ahimelek if he had a weapon, he was told the sword of Goliath was there wrapped in a cloth behind the ephod. (1 Samuel 21:8 – 10). The sword of Goliath represented spoil from past victory that he never got to enjoy. The ephod is a symbol of the garment of praise. David takes the sword of his defeated enemy and heads for his homeland, which was Gath. David is going after what rightfully belonged to him

David heads to Gath – Why? That's where the enemy's wealth was located. David takes the sword of Goliath (The Spirit), wrapped in the ephod (Praise) and heads to the enemies camp! He is now moving in the anointing of Prophet, Priest, and King.

"Or else how can one enter into a strong man's house, and spoil his goods, except he first bind the strong man? and then he will spoil his house." Matthew 12:29

In Bible days when you defeated an enemy you got all of his wealth and riches. Goliath was a wealthy man, therefore all that he had was David's. No doubt he would need the wealth of his enemy to unite the kingdom of Israel, which is a representation of the kingdom that we are now in, the kingdom of God, through the blood of Jesus Christ. Don't you see that's what Jesus came to do? He came to take back all the enemy has stolen. David is an Old Testament picture of the New Testament truth.

What did Jesus really mean when he said, *"For the Son of Man has come to seek and to save that which was lost?"* (See Luke 19:10). Most of us have been taught that Jesus was simply talking about salvation, right? Of course, salvation is a part, but not the whole. Taking the totality of his teaching Jesus was saying... *"I am here to establish the kingdom, and to regain what was lost. I am willing to shed my blood and hang on a cross as the perfect sacrifice in order for the contract of dominion to be restored. Adam and Eve sold out, and I am here to take it back.* That's good news for you and me, and bad news for the devil!

We are told David was a man after God's own heart, why? Because David tapped into something hundreds of years before Jesus Christ ever walked on the earth and preached Kingdom revelation.

We sing and quote Scriptures that David wrote, not realizing that David wrote those Scriptures centuries before Jesus was born. We quote them like they are New Testament Scriptures, but in fact David wrote those verses long before Jesus revealed the truth about the kingdom of God.

In David's day, to get into the presence of God you had to bring a blood sacrifice. But, David said I've discovered a revelation. You don't have to have a blood sacrifice to get into

His presence. It's true, you have to have a blood sacrifice to get your sins forgiven, but to come into He is presence blood was not required.

David discovered the secret to worship. If you will enter His gates with thanksgiving, and His courts with praise, and be thankful unto Him and bless His holy name you will find out the Lord is good! David discovered the revelation before Jesus Christ ever died on the cross.

My friend, praising Jesus is the only thing left that can be done to Him. You can't do anything to Him that has not already been tried.

If you try to burn Him out – He will walk out of the fire without the smell of smoke. If you try to flood Him out – He will walk out on top of the water. If you try to blow Him out – He will just say peace be still. If you try to kill Him – He will get up in three days. ***HE IS WORTHY TO BE PRAISED!***

Make a joyful noise unto the Lord, all ye lands. Serve the Lord with gladness: come before his presence with singing. Know ye that the Lord he is God: it is he that hath made us, and not we ourselves; we are his people, and the sheep of his pasture. Enter into his gates with thanksgiving, and into his courts with praise: be thankful unto him, and bless his name. For the Lord is good; his mercy is everlasting; and his truth endureth to all generations. Psalm 100:1-5

It' time to put aside our petty preferences, and silly arguments. Jesus did not come to establish a religion, or might I say Christianity. No, a thousand times no! He came to take back stolen authority. What Adam and Eve gave away Jesus came to reclaim. If we really knew what power and authority was at our disposal we would never walk around defeated.

Oh, my dear friend, whatever you are hungry for He will give it to you. If you are physically hungry He will feed you. If you are hungry for healing He will heal you. If you are hungry for revelation He will shine His light into your spirit.

NOW, TURN THE PAGE

I love secrets, don't you? I don't know that I have ever met a person who didn't like to be *"In the know."* In the next chapter I am going to show you a Kingdom secret that will blow your mind (If it's not blown already). So, hang in, and turn the page. You won't regret it!

Chapter 6

I KNOW A SECRET

Another parable put he forth unto them, saying, The kingdom of heaven is likened unto a man which sowed good seed in his field: But while men slept, his enemy came and sowed tares among the wheat, and went his way. But when the blade was sprung up, and brought forth fruit, then appeared the tares also. So the servants of the householder came and said unto him, Sir, didst not thou sow good seed in thy field? from whence then hath it tares? He said unto them, An enemy hath done this. The servants said unto him, Wilt thou then that we go and gather them up? But he said, Nay; lest while ye gather up the tares, ye root up also the wheat with them. Let both grow together until the harvest: and in the time of harvest I will say to the reapers, Gather ye together first the tares, and bind them in bundles to burn them: but gather the wheat into my barn. Matthew 13:24-30

I want to give you a heads up. The next three chapters are an information overload. If you enjoy the depth of God's word, then brace yourself, you're in for quite a ride.

The parable of the wheat and tares is a profound truth. It goes like this: A farmer sowed good seed on good ground, but while he slept an enemy came and sowed tares among the wheat.

When his workers realized what had been done they asked the farmer if they should begin removing the tares, and he said no, it's easier to tell the difference at harvest time. We'll bring the wheat into the barn, but we'll separate the tares into bundles and burn them.

The disciples came and asked Him to explain the

meaning. The interpretation is found in verses 36-42:

Then Jesus sent the multitude away, and went into the house: and his disciples came unto him, saying, Declare unto us the parable of the tares of the field. He answered and said unto them, He that soweth the good seed is the Son of man; The field is the world; the good seed are the children of the kingdom; but the tares are the children of the wicked one; The enemy that sowed them is the devil; the harvest is the end of the world; and the reapers are the angels. As therefore the tares are gathered and burned in the fire; so shall it be in the end of this world The Son of man shall send forth his angels, and they shall gather out of his kingdom all things that offend, and them which do iniquity; And shall cast them into a furnace of fire: there shall be wailing and gnashing of teeth.

Jesus explained it this way:

"He that sowed a good seed was me."

"The field is the world."

"The good seed is the children of the kingdom."

"Tares are the children of the wicked one."

"The enemy that sowed the tares was the devil."

"The harvest is the end of the world."

"The reapers are the Angels."

"Therefore, the tares are gathered and burned in the fire, so shall it be at the end of this world."

HE SPOKE IN PARABLES

There are times we read events in the Scripture, especially in the New Testament, as isolated events. Matthew 13 is simply a continuation of a 24 hour period in which certain events are recorded in the ministry of Jesus Christ. Up until this point His teaching was direct and to the point. In Matthew 13 Jesus used a different method of teaching. The religious crowd was plotting to stop Him. So, what did He do? He chose the use of parables to explain to his disciples the "inside story" concerning The Kingdom of God.

The Greek word for parable is *"parabole"* means *"to cast alongside."* It is the placing of things side-by-side with the intention of explaining one by the other. It is a story, or a comparison that is put alongside something else to help make the meaning clear.

The Caldwell translation puts it this way: *"a simple everyday story that has a heavenly meaning."*

In Matthew 13 Jesus told seven parables to reveal the mysteries of the Kingdom. A *"mystery"* is a spiritual truth understood by divine revelation. Jesus spoke in parables, and according to Matthew He is **revealing things that have been kept secret from the foundation of the world.** Everybody likes secrets. It's just human nature to want to be "in the know."

All these things spake Jesus unto the multitude in parables; and without a parable spake he not unto them: That it might be fulfilled which was spoken by the prophet, saying, I will open my mouth in parables; I will utter things which have been kept secret from the foundation of the world. Matthew 13:34-35

I will open my mouth in a parable: I will utter dark sayings of old: Psalm 78:2

Why would God "hide" things? Remember, I already shared with you in an earlier chapter (See chapter 2) the meaning of Proverbs 25:2: *"It is the glory of God to conceal a thing: but the honour of kings is to search out a matter."*

I am not going to repeat it all here but, I remind you the essence of what Solomon said: *"it is the glory of God to conceal His Word* <u>*or revelatory things of His Word*</u>*, but it is the honor of Kings, (which represents you and I) to search out that word. God loves to conceal things."*

"Well, Brother Caldwell why didn't God just tell us plain out?" I'll tell you why. He gets a kick out of hiding a revelatory word in His Word. The word *"conceal"* means *"the intent of provoking someone to seek."* He enjoys hiding things. There is no reason to hide something if no one is going to seek it. Once you know that God has your best interest at heart, and God is hiding things in His Word for you and I to search out then you can better understand the mysteries of the Kingdom. God loves to conceal things so those who know His spirit can search it out. Once you have been redeemed, washed in the blood of Jesus, your spiritual hearing is open to receive the revelation of the

kingdom of God.

I am convinced Satan does not know what God is hiding in His Word because God's ways are past finding out. If Satan knew everything God was going to do for you he would try his best to sabotage what God has planned. Therefore, God hides His promises, His word in His word, wanting to provoke you to seek it out to keep Satan from trying to head off the blessing that God has in store for you!

WHAT IS A TARE?

To understand God's plan I believe you have to go to the wheat and the tares. Jesus said this is what the kingdom is like. After Jesus told the parable he sent the multitude away. I think it is interesting and significant that later on when the disciples asked the Lord to explain this parable to them you will notice they don't say anything about the wheat. They said, *"Lord, what is the parable of the tares?"* Now the parable was a parable of the wheat and the tares, the good and the bad. But what stuck in their minds was, *"Give us an explanation of the tares."*

I had no idea what a tare was, so I had the opportunity to talk to a wheat farmer up in Kansas. I knew if anybody could explain it, he could.

I said, *"Explain something to me. What is a tare?"*

He said, *"Brother Randy, A tare is nothing more than empty wheat."* When he said that I knew there had to be more. I asked him to give me a few more details.

He explained. *"When you take the grain, what Jesus calls the corn of wheat, and you take the grain of a tare and lay them side by side they look exactly the same. Even the trained eye cannot look at them and tell you which one is a tare and which one is wheat. But, there is a real difference if you know what to look for. The real wheat is heavy and it's dense and you can do many things with it. But, the tare is just the outside. There is nothing on the inside."*

I said, *"How can you tell them apart?"*

Well, Brother Caldwell you can't until the harvest time. Or, when the wind starts to blow. When the wind starts to blow across the field the real grain will bow, but the tare will stand erect!"

So, here's the deal. The tares act like wheat and they look like wheat, but this is where the similarities end. One thing the tare cannot produce is fruit. If you were to open the head of a wheat plant, you would find it filled with wheat kernels. If you opened the head of the tare, you would find it filled with tiny black seeds. A tare is nothing more than a poisonous weed. I am told if you try to eat it or feed it to your livestock you could actually cause harm. It can cause nausea, convulsions, and if enough is eaten, even death!

Satan loves to counterfeit the real! You know as well as I you can't counterfeit something unless you have the real to compare it to. How do you suppose bank tellers are trained to

96

identify counterfeit money? They are so familiar with the real thing that when the counterfeit shows up they can spot it a mile away. A good counterfeit may look like the real thing, and it may feel like the real thing to most people. But, those who have been trained know how to spot the fake. They can see it, feel it, and reject it!

Satan has:

- Counterfeit Christians (2 Corinthians 11:26).
- A counterfeit Gospel (Galatians 1:6-9).
- A counterfeit Righteousness (Romans 10:1-3).
- A counterfeit Church (Revelation 2:9).
- And, will produce a counterfeit Christ (2 Thessalonians 2:1-12).

It is interesting to note the response of the farmer when he was asked about the removal of the tares. His counsel was to allow them both to grow together until the harvest. Why? *"Lest while ye gather up the tares, ye root up also the wheat with them. Let both grow together until the harvest: and in the time of harvest I will say to the reapers, Gather ye together first the tares, and bind them in bundles to burn them:"*

You see, the roots of the tares would intertwine with those of the wheat and if the tares were pulled out, then some of the wheat would be damaged also. Our job is not to go around and pull the tares. That's His job at harvest time!

I believe the story of the wheat and the tares is like the beginning of the world. The counterfeit spirit, which is the spirit of antichrist, didn't just show up when Jesus did. It's been around since the Garden of Eden.

In Genesis 1-5 you will find creation, and the reorganization of planet earth. You read where God told Adam and Eve to take responsibility over the Garden. He told them to dress it, tend it, and keep it. In other words, He told them to protect it at all cost.

No doubt the Garden of Eden was the most beautiful spot on planet Earth. It was created to be man's ideal environment. It was literally the place where God's presence touched down, the one place on earth where God's presence dwelt. It was specifically designed for God and man to have unbroken fellowship.

Listed among the beauty of the garden you will find the Tree of Life. If you fast forward to the book of Revelation you will also find in the New Jerusalem the Tree of Life. Everything that is listed in the Garden of Eden you will find listed in the New Jerusalem except one thing – *The Tree of Knowledge of Good and Evil.*

Keep in mind Jesus is revealing things kept secret from the foundation of the world. He is telling the parable of the wheat and tares. Is it possible God gave Adam the garden and told him to tend it, protect it, and yet while Adam was sleeping the enemy sowed bad seed in the garden?

The reason I suggest this is because I have trouble buying the philosophy God put man in an ideal environment and tempted him with the Tree of Knowledge of Good and Evil.

We all love our children and grandchildren. Can you imagine preparing a wonderful meal for your child, setting them at the table and pointing out all the delicious things they can enjoy? You say to them, *"You can have anything you want with the exception of the one bowl of fruit I set by your plate. The fruit contains strychnine. Whatever you do don't drip it on your food because it will kill you!"* You say, *"Brother Randy that is silly!"* I would agree with you one hundred percent. But, somehow we suggest that is exactly what a loving God did In the Garden of Eden. I believe I have enough solid Scripture to stand on to prove my case.

Now the serpent was more subtil than any beast of the field which the Lord God had made. And he said unto the woman, Yea, hath God said, Ye shall not eat of every tree of the garden? And the woman said unto the serpent, We may eat of the fruit of the trees of the garden: But of the fruit of the tree which is in the midst of the garden, God hath said, Ye shall not eat of it, neither shall ye touch it, lest ye die. And the serpent said unto the woman, Ye shall not surely die: For God doth know that in the day ye eat thereof, then your eyes shall be opened, and ye shall be as gods, knowing good and evil. And when the woman saw that the tree was good for food, and that it was pleasant to the eyes, and a tree to be desired to make one wise, she took of the fruit thereof, and did eat, and gave also unto her husband with her; and he did eat. **Genesis 3:1-6**

The word "subtle" is more probably best translated in today's English as *"slick."* So the serpent was the slickest beast God made. We know of course it is Satan hiding underneath his mask. Two other times in Scripture we hear him talking (Job 1:9; Matthew 4:3).

When the "slick one" wanted to deceive Eve into sin he did not attack her physically, but mentally. The apostle Paul made that very clear in 2 Corinthians 11:3.... **"But I fear, lest by any means, as the serpent beguiled Eve through his subtilty, so your minds should be corrupted from the simplicity that is in Christ."** And, again in 1 Timothy 2:14... *"And Adam was not deceived, but the woman being deceived was in the transgression."*

Why would he attack her through her mind? I believe it's because our mind is a part of the image of God. It is where God communicates with you.

And be not conformed to this world: but be ye transformed by the renewing of your mind, that ye may prove what is that good, and acceptable, and perfect, will of God (Romans 12:2).

Our lives are renewed through the renewing of our mind. Our minds are renewed through the truth of God's word (John

17:17). The purpose of the "slick one" is to cause you to believe a lie. If a lie can worm its way into your life, then sin is not far behind. If we know he attacks our mind then we must protect it at all cost.

Finally, brethren, whatsoever things are true, whatsoever things are honest, whatsoever things are just, whatsoever things are pure, whatsoever things are lovely, whatsoever things are of good report; if there be any virtue, and if there be any praise, think on these things. Philippians 4:8

Now watch how Satan approached Eve, and caused her to believe his lie.

1. He caused her to <u>doubt God's</u> word. "*Yea, hath God said.*" He sowed seeds of doubt, and in turn Eve misquotes God.

- She misquoted God's permission. God told them in chapter 2:16... *"Of every tree of the garden thou mayest freely eat."* Eve left out the fact God told them they had free reign to eat and enjoy everything He provided for them. When you start to misquote God's grace *(freely is a picture of grace)* it becomes much easier to disobey the will of God.

- She misquoted God's <u>prohibition </u>in verse 3... "***But of the fruit of the tree which is in the midst of the garden, God hath said, Ye shall not eat of it, neither shall ye touch it, lest ye die.*** God never told them

101

not to touch the tree. Like a spoiled child Eve stuck out her lower lip and said, *"We can't even touch the tree, or God is going to kill us."* I mean really, is that what God told them? Absolutely not!

- She misquoted God's penalty. ***"God hath said, Ye shall not eat of it, neither shall ye touch it, lest ye die.*** She left out an important word God had spoken in 2:17... ***"For in the day that thou eatest thereof thou shalt surely die."*** Satan made it sound like the penalty was not very harsh. God made it abundantly clear the penalty was death, and he did not put a question mark behind it!"

2. He <u>denied</u> God's word. *"Ye shall not surely die."*

It did not take much to go from doubting God's word to denying God's word. It's almost as if the "slick one" said to Eve, *"You need to really consider if that is what God really meant?"* Satan was not denying the fact God had spoken to them. He was just hinting that God would never really cause them to suffer any kind of penalty.

3. He caused her to <u>doubt</u> God's love. *"For God doth know that in the day ye eat thereof, then your eyes shall be opened, and ye shall be as gods, knowing good and evil."*

His seeds of deception were so subtle Eve missed it altogether. *"If God really cared for you He would not deny you anything. After all, how could a loving God keep anything from you?"* You will notice it is not God, but *"gods."* The word in Hebrew means: *"Someone who is an extension of, speaking for; or we might say like an ambassador."*

Satan hints God is holding out on you. If you eat the fruit you will be able to speak on His behalf. How big of a liar is the devil? He was offering something she already had. Eve already had that position!

How subtle is Satan? He did not show up in his true character, nor did he say to Eve, *"I am about to lie to you."* No, he approached Eve wearing a mask, and simply began to question God. He will always accomplish his purposes through lies. God will accomplish His purposes through the truth. Be careful my friend when you begin to believe the lies of the enemy. That is when "the father of lies" (John 8:44) will go to work to destroy you!

We are specifically warned in the book of Revelation how to treat the word of God.

For I testify unto every man that heareth the words of the prophecy of this book, If any man shall add unto these things, God shall add unto him the plagues that are written in this book: And if any man shall take away from the words of the book of this prophecy, God shall take away his part out of the book of life, and out of the holy city, and from the things which are written in this book. Revelation 22:18-19

This is pretty serious Scripture. God says if you add to

what I'm saying I am going to add plagues to you, and if you take away from what I'm saying I am going to take your name out of the book of life. God is very clear about people twisting His Word. We are 6000 years removed from the Garden of Eden and God is still upset about the distortion of His word. At the end of the book of Revelation God issues a warning – *"Don't do it!"*

When you take the Word of God and twist it to justify a disobedient lifestyle you have swallowed the lie of the enemy. When the Holy Ghost points out things in your life that are in error, and you try to justify your response by misquoting the word of God you are operating in the spirit of antichrist.

Cain And Abel Go To Church – The Spirit Of Antichrist Is Alive And Well!

And Adam knew Eve his wife; and she conceived, and bare Cain, and said, I have gotten a man from the Lord. And she again bare his brother Abel. And Abel was a keeper of sheep, but Cain was a tiller of the ground. And in process of time it came to pass, that Cain brought of the fruit of the ground an offering unto the Lord. And Abel, he also brought of the firstlings of his flock and of the fat thereof. And the Lord had respect unto Abel and to his offering: But unto Cain and to his offering he had not respect. And Cain was very wroth, and his countenance fell And the Lord said unto Cain, Why art thou wroth? and why is thy countenance fallen? If thou doest well, shalt thou not be accepted? and if thou doest not well, sin lieth at the door. And unto thee shall be his desire, and thou shalt rule over him. Genesis 4:1-7

Adam and Eve had two boys, Cain and Abel. As these twin boys began to grow the Bible said Able was a keeper of the sheep, while Cain was a tiller of the ground.

It was obvious these boys were taught that when you go to church you bring an offering. You don't come to worship empty-handed. The word for offering in Verse 3 is "minchah." The word is used to describe BOTH offerings, not just Cain's offering from the ground. For years I have heard people say when God kicked Adam and Eve out of the garden He cursed them. Only one thing wrong with that, it's just flat out wrong! God did not curse Adam and Eve. God cursed the ground, and He cursed the serpent. If God cursed the ground then the fruit of the ground is cursed, right? Cain brought a "minchah" offering to God. Abel also brought the firstlings of his flock as an offering to God.

Now watch. *"And the Lord had respect unto Abel and to his offering (minchah): But unto Cain and to his offering (minchah) he had not respect."* As I began to examine this verse I was amazed to discover Cain and Abel brought the exact same offering to God. You say, *"Now wait a minute Brother Caldwell, are you sure about that?" I am absolutely positive!*

Both of these boys brought a grain offering a "minchah" to the Lord. But, that is all Cain brought. Abel, along with his "minchah" offering brought the firstlings of the flock, and the fat thereof. Why? Because Abel understood God had cursed the ground. I cannot bring an offering to God that has a curse on it. There is no doubt in my mind at some point these brothers were taught to bring an innocent lamb sacrifice to cover the curse (Genesis 3:21). One did and was blessed. One didn't and was rejected!

By faith Abel offered unto God a more excellent sacrifice than Cain, by which he obtained witness that he was righteous, God testifying of his gifts: and by it he being dead yet speaketh. Hebrews 11:4

To say that Cain was unhappy is an understatement. *"And Cain was very wroth, and his countenance fell And the Lord said unto Cain, Why art thou wroth? and why is thy countenance fallen?"* He was mad. He didn't get his way. I can almost hear him say, *"We both brought the same offering, and it's just not fair!"*

The Lord said, *"Dude, why are you so mad? What are you so bent out of shape about? You know good and well if you do what is right you will be accepted. If you don't do what is right sin is laying at the door waiting on you."* (Caldwell translation)

Cain was not a misguided youth. Cain was moving in the first antichrist spirit to tear down a fellowship. God gave him an opportunity to straighten up. But, instead of obeying God he commits the first murder in the Bible.

And Cain talked with Abel his brother: and it came to

106

pass, when they were in the field, that Cain rose up against Abel his brother, and slew him. And the Lord said unto Cain, Where is Abel thy brother? And he said, I know not: Am I my brother's keeper? And he said, What hast thou done? the voice of thy brother's blood crieth unto me from the ground.and now art thou cursed from the earth, which hath opened her mouth to receive thy brother's blood from thy hand; When thou tillest the ground, it shall not henceforth yield unto thee her strength; a fugitive and a vagabond shalt thou be in the earth. And Cain said unto the Lord, My punishment is greater than I can bear. Behold, thou hast driven me out this day from the face of the earth; and from thy face shall I be hid; and I shall be a fugitive and a vagabond in the earth; and it shall come to pass, that every one that findeth me shall slay me. And the Lord said unto him, Therefore whosoever slayeth Cain, vengeance shall be taken on him sevenfold. And the Lord set a mark upon Cain, lest any finding him should kill him. And Cain went out from the presence of the Lord, and dwelt in the land of Nod, on the east of Eden. Genesis 4:8-16

It is obvious that Cain did not repent though God cursed him and everything he touched. If you are a farmer and the ground is not yielding its fruit you have a big problem.

SIN WILL ALWAYS LEAVE A MARK!

Cain had remorse but not repentance. He had complaint but not conversion. He was filled with fear but not faith. "*and from thy face shall I be hid; and I shall be a fugitive and a vagabond in the earth;"* The phrase "from thy face" means the presence of God. Cain became a wanderer and a vagabond, without a home, and without the presence of God. According to Jude he was nothing more than a *"wandering star" (Jude 11).*

He is now consigned to roam the earth bearing a physical scar, a mark, so people could recognize who he was. God put a physical mark on him so the people would not confuse the true spirit of Christ with the spirit of antichrist. Cain became the first tare among the wheat.

Why in the world did Cain not listen to the Lord and do what was right? 1 John 3:12 says, *"Not as Cain, who was of that wicked one, and slew his brother. And wherefore slew he him? Because his own works were evil, and his brother's righteous."* Cain was of the seed of the wicked one, why? Because whom you listen to becomes your father. Satan was not his biological father but his influence (lies) was stronger than the influence of the Lord.

In the New Testament, Jesus looked at the religious crowd (the spirit of antichrist) and declared *"If God were your Father, ye would love me: for I proceeded forth and came from God; neither came I of myself, but he sent me. Why do ye not understand my speech? Even because ye cannot hear my word. <u>Ye are of your father the devil</u>, and the lusts of your father ye will do. He was a murderer from the beginning, and abode not in the truth, because there is no truth in him. When he* *speaketh a lie, he speaketh of his own: for he is a liar, and the father of it. (John 8:42-44)* Again, Satan was not the actual biological father of this group so what did Jesus mean? They had received the word of Satan, and received the seed of lies sown into their life.

It does matter what you allow into your spirit. God intends for you to receive a "word" and good fruit grow from you. That won't happen unless the fallow ground is constantly broken up to receive the seed (Matthew 13:1-23).

Satan is the "prince of the power of the air" (Ephesians 2:2), which means there is "power in the air." Every type of communication you receive has to come through the air. If Satan is the prince, which is the position of the ruler of the power of the air, he has control over the power that is in the air, correct? That being true you have to be careful what you receive. Whether it's coming through a preacher, a television set, or cell phone – no matter the method, you better be careful.

That might explain how it's possible for five people, sitting on the same row, can hear me preach in a meeting and four of them say *"that was a powerful word."* And, the fifth one says, *"I didn't like it at all. It didn't do a thing for me, and besides I didn't like the way he parted his hair. I am mad and I am not coming back!"*

Could it be possible that negative response doesn't have anything to do with the speaker? Somewhere between my mouth and his hearing the "seed of the Word" was falling on hard ground. Could it be possible when the words leave my mouth, and before they get to his ear the prince of the power of the air takes them, twist them, and he "hears" them like it was never intended?

Don't Be Deceived

My whole life I have heard about the antichrist. I remember my father said they thought he was going to be Adolf Hitler. When things didn't work out for Hitler it started a long line of possible candidates. From John Kennedy all the way up until the present hour each generation has pointed the finger at some world leader and said, *"Surely he is the antichrist."*

Question? Why in the world has so many men in history appeared to be the antichrist? Because any one of them could have been. You see, Jesus said he's coming back and before He comes back the man of sin, the son of perdition, has to be revealed. Satan does not know when Jesus is coming back, so for two thousand years he has groomed some world leader to become the antichrist in case Jesus came back!

I think it's time to stop chasing after some world figure and realize it's not about a "person" but a "spirit." I don't think there is any one particular person that is designated to be the antichrist. The antichrist spirit is alive and well in a system of anti-God government, religion, and education. There will be a figurehead of all of this, but he will not be revealed until Jesus returns. So the best thing to do is to stop buying the latest video, or the latest book. Save your money, and stick your face in the Word of God.

It's time to allow the good seed of the word of God to be planted into the prepared soil of our heart. If you don't tune your spiritual hearing to what the Spirit is saying today you could possibly be deceived by the spirit of antichrist. God put a physical mark on Cain so the good seed could recognize what the enemy had done. In telling this parable Jesus revealed a mystery (something that has been hidden from the foundation of the world) to warn us.

The spirit of antichrist has been here from the beginning! When you understand the parable of the wheat and tares, the spirit of antichrist mingling among the good seed, you will not be deceived when the tares show up.

To understand the mysteries (a sacred secret) you have to experience the new birth. It doesn't come through education, joining the church, or giving money to your local charity.

In the next chapter I am going to show you the only way to "enter" the Kingdom is through a new birth. The new birth is not chosen from an à la carte menu of spiritual experiences. It is not one of many we can choose. It is a requirement to "know" and "understand" the hidden mysteries of the Kingdom of God.

Chapter 7

BORN INTO THE KINGDOM

There was a man of the Pharisees, named Nicodemus, a ruler of the Jews: The same came to Jesus by night, and said unto him, Rabbi, we know that thou art a teacher come from God: for no man can do these miracles that thou doest, except God be with him. Jesus answered and said unto him, Verily, verily, I say unto thee, except a man be born again, he cannot see the kingdom of God. Nicodemus saith unto him, how can a man be born when he is old? Can he enter the second time into his mother's womb, and be born. Jesus answered, Verily, verily, I say unto thee, except a man be born of water and of the Spirit, he cannot enter into the kingdom of God. That which is born of the flesh is flesh; and that which is born of the Spirit is spirit. Marvel not that I said unto thee, Ye must be born again. John 3:1-7

God has always had a plan. His original plan was not for you to "get saved" and go to heaven, but to extend His kingdom influence on the earth.

His desire is to have kingdom citizens who live by kingdom principles. He is not looking for more church members, but sons, citizens, and ambassadors who know and understand how to walk in rulership. He extends rulership (not ownership) to those of us who are willing to walk in kingdom authority. We need to change our focus from trying to get out of here to taking back everything the enemy has stolen. The devil loves it when we sing "I'll fly away," because he knows as long as we are trying to fly off the planet he can continue to exercise control over the planet!

Jesus spent 96% of his teaching time on the Kingdom of God, and how to pay for it. God never intended for the Kingdom to be funded by cake walks and chili suppers. I am not trying to demean any woman who is ever made quilts, baked a cake, or got up at 4 o'clock in the morning to cook for a pancake breakfast. I thank God for anyone willing to do their part, it has kept the church afloat for decades.

I think you would have to agree with me that any time you spend 96% on any subject that is your main focus. The other 4% Jesus talked about salvation, crucifixion, resurrection, healing, and peace of mind. Does that mean the 4% are trivial matters? No, it just means we have missed the main point of why He came, and what it really means to be an Ambassador of the Kingdom. Once you understand the message of the Gospel of the Kingdom everything else makes sense.

Brother Caldwell, are you saying that we should not teach about salvation, and being born again?

I'm not saying that at all, of course it is important to teach about being born again. It's not a trivial matter. It is how you get into the kingdom!

You don't enter the kingdom by joining the church. Our churches are filled with "members in good standing" who don't have a clue what it means to walk in Kingdom authority. For them it's enough to come to church, hear a sermon, give a little (emphasis on "little") money and go home.

You don't join the kingdom, you are born into the

kingdom! I am shocked when I talk to people about the Kingdom. I get a blank stare sometimes, and the only answer I get is... *"Oh, Brother Caldwell I have always been a Christian. I was brought to the church two weeks after I was born. I was literally raised on the pew. My daddy was a deacon, and my mother was the head of the Women's Missionary Group. I don't need all that born again stuff, I am just fine."*

If all there is to the Kingdom of God is being a good church member, or being raised in the church then my friend we might as well pack it in and call it a day! I don't mean to burst your bubble, but Jesus has something to say about it.

Let's break down John chapter 3 and discover amazing truth about entering the Kingdom of God.

WHAT DOES IT MEAN TO BE "BORN AGAIN?"

When people claim they have been born again what does it really mean? It is a legitimate Bible term used by Jesus to describe an experience that each person must have. Every individual – every man, every woman, every boy and girl needs to experience what Jesus described as being born again.

I find it interesting this is the only time Jesus talked about being born again. He never mentioned it to a large congregation of people. The only time he talked about it was to a man at 3 o'clock in the morning, who apparently was not even looking to be born again. Nicodemus did not come to ask about being saved. He came to Jesus to ask about the Kingdom. Every time he asked Jesus a question, or made a statement, Jesus brought him right back to the necessity of the new birth.

Although Jesus did not talk about it again there are several references in the New Testament describing the same experience: *"But as many as received him, to them gave He power to become the sons of God, even to them that believe on his name: Which were born, not of blood, nor of the will of the flesh, nor of the will of man, but of God." John 1:12-13*

James wrote about being born again in James 1:18, *"Of his own will begat he us with the word of truth."*

In 1 Peter 1:23, *"Being born again, not of corruptible seed, but of incorruptible, by the word of God, which liveth and abideth for ever."*

This is just Bible terminology describing an experience we call "the new birth" or regeneration. Don't be afraid of the word *regeneration.* It's just another way of describing a rebirth.

John the Baptist, the forerunner of Jesus Christ, declared in Matthew 3:2, *"Repent ye: for the kingdom of heaven is at hand."* John looked straight into the eyes of the religious crowd and told them repentance was the first step toward the kingdom.

How many times have people flocked to the altar to supposedly "repent" and yet their lives never change? How do you know when someone has really repented? Is it how loud they scream and cry at the altar? Is it how long they talk to the pastor in a counseling session? To repent is to change your way of thinking which leads to a changed of behavior. I can tell you how you can know if real Bible repentance has taken place – it's when you are put in the same position that got you in trouble the first time and you make a different decision! Crying at the altar does not produce change. It is nothing more than whitewashing the outside of the gravestone. It is "just putting a new suit on an old man." Being born again is putting "a new man in an old suit."

We have had enough of reformation, what we need is regeneration. Reformation is putting lipstick on a pig! You can clean that old pig up, give its tail a new curl, put a ribbon in her hair, and sit her in front of the TV and let her watch Oprah and Dr. Phil all day long. But I guarantee you, as soon as she goes outside and walks by a mud puddle she is going to jump in head first! Why? It's just her nature. You don't change a pig's nature on the outside. It has never happened, and it never will.

"Therefore if any man be in Christ, he is a new creature: old things are passed away; behold, all things are become new." 2 Corinthians 5:17

The new birth experience is not cleaning us up on the outside but it's changing us from the inside.

Enter Nicodemus – Who was this man who came to Jesus?

"There was a man of the Pharisees, named Nicodemus, a ruler of the Jews:"

Three times Nicodemus walked across the pages of Scripture.

116

- In John 3 he desires to talk to Jesus. (3:1-7)
- In John 7 he defends Jesus. (7:50-53)
- In John 19 he displays devotion to Jesus. (19:39)

Nicodemus came to the Lord "by night." There are many Bible scholars who believe it was around 3 o'clock in the morning. For John to emphasize the time of his visit indicates the reason he came at such an odd time was because he did not want anyone to know he was there. It may be he did not want to be seen by the religious crowd.

John gives us no explanation what Nicodemus came looking for, except for the obvious fact that he must have been curious about all this "Kingdom talk." It appeared Jesus answered a question Nicodemus did not ask. It could be that John picked up the middle part of the conversation so we are left to wonder how it all started.

Nicodemus continued the conversation with a compliment, and a concession.

"and said unto him, Rabbi, we know that thou art a teacher come from God: for no man can do these miracles that thou doest, except God be with him."

Jesus did not even respond but simply said... *"verily, verily, I say unto thee, except a man be born again, he cannot see the kingdom of God."* Jesus sets before this religious leader the absolute necessity of being born again. The word *"see"* means to *"perceive or to know."* Unless you are born again you don't know that the Kingdom actually exist. Later in the

117

conversation Jesus added this...*"Except a man be born of water and of the Spirit, he cannot enter into the kingdom of God.* The word "enter" does mean to "walk inside," it means to *"enjoy the benefits of."* Nicodemus before you can *"perceive or know the Kingdom, and enjoy its benefits, you must be born again!"*

This is an amazing statement considering who Nicodemus was. It must have been a shock to his system when Jesus did not respond to his obvious attempt to gain favor. This was no ordinary guy who just showed up to see what all the fuss was about.

- He was a highly <u>respected man.</u>

His name is a Greek name. It was a common custom among the Jews for the parents to give their boys two names, a Jewish and a Gentile name. You can see that in the case of the apostle Paul. His Jewish name was Saul, and his Gentile name was Paul.

Nicodemus is made up of two words, a word which means *"to conquer,"* and one which means *"the common people."* The total word means *"One who conquers the people."* His name fits perfectly with the tradition of the Pharisees which included the idea they were above the common people. They lived out a perfect definition of religious class warfare! They were above, the people were beneath. They had a direct line to heaven, and the people had to go through them to find out what God thought about them.

If you want to see what Jesus thought about the religious

spirit just read Matthew 23. He blistered them because of the heavy burden they placed on the backs of the people in the form of religious do's and don'ts. I have told you over and over again God hates religion – it stinks!

- He was a <u>religious man</u>.

We are told he was a ruler of the Jews. The word "ruler" is the Greek word *"archon,"* which means, *"the chief one, ruler, or prince."* This word is used to describe the rulers of the local synagogues, and members of the Sanhedrin. The Sanhedrin was the religious Supreme Court of the Jewish people. He was prominent, influential, and very wealthy. There is a tradition that says Nicodemus was one of the three richest men in Jerusalem.

To be a Pharisee meant more than just being a religious person. The word "Pharisee" means *"the separated ones."* A Pharisee was a man who viewed himself separated by God for divine purposes; a Pharisee was extremely fanatical in his service to God. Looking back we can see the hypocrisy of the Pharisees. But, in that day they were considered the most religious and committed leaders in Israel. The Pharisees believed in the supernatural, as opposed to the other religious group of the day, the Sadducees, who did not believe in anything supernatural. It would be safe to say the Pharisees were the conservatives of the day in the Sadducees were the liberals.

He was as religious as you could possibly be, and yet with all of his religion he still did not know about the new birth. I find it amazing because in the book of Ezekiel the prophet talks

119

about getting a new heart (Ezekiel 11:19). It seems to me with all of his theological training and religious upbringing he would have known what the prophet was talking about. Jesus said, *"how can you be a master in Israel and not knowest about these things?"*

The Caldwell translation of what Jesus said to him is, *"Nicodemus, how can you be so smart and so dumb at the same time? Read your Bible dummy and you will see throughout the Old Testament the Prophets were pointing to a "new birth" experience!"*

It is obvious Jesus was not afraid to confront this religious leader with the necessity of being born from above. He would not be the first or the last religious person to realize that with all their religion it would not be enough to enter the kingdom of God. He was a prominent and respected man in the city of Jerusalem, and yet Jesus brushed aside all of his respectability and told him he had a need. Nicodemus would not be the first guy to think his community service and accomplishments in religion would get him favor with God.

You might be thinking, *"Brother Randy, don't you think Jesus was a little tough on this guy? After all, he was one of the most prominent men of his day? Shouldn't Jesus have been more careful not to offend him? Maybe it would have been better if Jesus engaged him in a' dialogue' and invited him down to one of his meetings?"*

My answer is simply- *NO!* I don't think that at all. Jesus

120

was not interested in his many accomplishments, nor was he impressed with all of his education. Nothing wrong with accomplishments and education, but it will not substitute for the new birth. The Bible states all have sinned and come short of the glory of God (Romans 3:23). Jesus was not giving Nicodemus a suggestion, a hint, or a gentle reminder. No exceptions, and no excuses, you must be born again! Jesus was not impressed with what he had, or who he was, He simply said to him, *"Ye must be born again!"*

WHY WAS JESUS SO DOGMATIC?

We are all born with a sinful nature, and something had to be done. David wrote in Psalm 51:5, *"Behold, I was shapen in iniquity; and in sin did my mother conceive me.*

Don't misunderstand me. David was not saying the act of conception is a sin, but we were born with a sinful nature. You and I were born wrong the first time, so we need a second birth. Only the new birth can change the human heart.

Jesus answered and said unto him, Verily, verily, I say unto thee, except a man be born again, he cannot see the kingdom of God.

In order to enter the Kingdom, and enjoy its benefits, and know kingdom mysteries the new birth is an absolute necessity. The natural mind (the one you are born with) can never understand the things of God. I believe this is what Peter was talking about when he said, *"We are a partaker of the divine nature."*

Nicodemus saith unto him, how can a man be born when he is old? Can he enter the second time into his mother's womb, and be born.

Nicodemus asked a very logical question. How can I go back into my mother's womb and be born a second time? I think Nicodemus was probably an old guy, and he was saying, *"I am an old man, and although I wish I could, there is no way I could start all over again."* He must have been excited about the prospect of starting over, but he was puzzled about how it would happen.

BIRTH BRINGS LIFE

Nicodemus was a man who had no eyes to see spiritual truth, and no heart to feel the presence of God in his life. Jesus said in order to experience the kingdom you have to be born from above. The moment that happens spiritual life begins to pulsate through your being.

John wrote in his first epistle (5:12*): "He that hath the Son hath life, and he that hath not the Son of God hath not life."*

When a baby is born birth takes place. Your car does not have life because it was manufactured, and not born. Babies have life because babies are born. To be born spiritually means you have received life that you did not have before!

Jesus compared the new birth to a physical birth...*"Except a man be born of water and of the Spirit, he cannot enter into the kingdom of God. That which is born of the flesh is flesh; and that which is born of the Spirit is spirit. "*

There are some who say the reference to "water" is just talking about the physical process of birth. There are others who believe He was referring to water baptism. It's all right with me if you want to believe any of that, but I believe it is referring to the "Word" of God.

"That he might sanctify and cleanse it with the washing of water by the word." Ephesians 5:26

Birth involves two parents, a mother and a father. Being born again involves the "water of the Word, and the Spirit of God. And again I quote 1 Peter1:23, "*Being born again, not of corruptible seed, but of incorruptible, by the word of God, which liveth and abideth for ever.* The Spirit of God takes the Word of God and produces a child of God!

EZEKIEL LOOKED FORWARD TO THIS DAY

Ezekiel, a prophet of God, talked about the nation of Israel. More than likely we know him from his prophecies about the Valley of dry bones (Ezekiel 37). In chapter 16 he writes about the birth of the nation. You may read that chapter and wonder how it applies to us especially since we are talking about the new birth?

Again the word of the Lord came unto me, saying, Son of man, cause Jerusalem to know her abominations, And say, Thus saith the Lord God unto Jerusalem; Thy birth and thy nativity is of the land of Canaan; thy father was an Amorite, and thy mother an Hittite. And as for thy nativity, in the day thou wast born thy navel was not cut, neither wast thou washed in water to supple thee; thou wast not salted at all, nor swaddled at all. None eye pitied thee, to do any of these unto thee, to have compassion upon thee; but thou wast cast out in the open field, to the lothing of thy person, in the day that thou wast born. And when I passed by thee, and saw thee polluted in thine own blood, I said unto thee when thou wast in thy blood, Live; yea, I said unto thee when thou wast in thy blood, Live. I have caused thee to multiply as the bud of the field, and thou hast increased and waxen great, and thou art come to excellent ornaments: thy breasts are fashioned, and thine hair is grown, whereas thou wast naked and bare. Now when I passed by thee, and looked upon thee, behold, thy time was the time of love; and I spread my skirt over thee, and covered thy nakedness: yea, I sware unto thee, and entered into a covenant with thee, saith the Lord God, and thou becamest mine. Then washed I thee with water; yea, I throughly washed away thy blood from thee, and I anointed thee with oil. Ezekiel 16:1-9.

Centuries before the conversation between Jesus and Nicodemus the prophet Ezekiel talked about the kingdom that is coming, "*Thus saith the Lord God unto Jerusalem; Thy birth*

and thy nativity is of the land of Canaan;" When they came into existence they were an orphan. Their navel was not cut.

When a woman has a baby they have to cut the umbilical cord. If you don't release the baby from where it came from, the baby will die and quite possibly kill the mother. Why? Because before the baby was delivered it received all of its nutrition and nourishment from the umbilical cord. Once it is delivered from what held it, it has to be cut. It can no longer be fed and receive nutrition from where it came from.

I can remember as a kid I used to hear people stand up in church and say, *"I am so glad that God delivered me from sin."* Even then I realized what they were saying. When you say *"I am glad I am born again and delivered from sin,"* you are actually making the statement there was a time you were bound in the "uterus of iniquity." I was in the womb of sin but the Great Physician came and brought me out of darkness and I was delivered from what held me captive.

The problem with a lot of people who go to church every Sunday is that they have been born again into the kingdom, but have never cut the umbilical cord. They are still trying to be fed from their past. The umbilical cord has never been cut!

God's plan for us is to take the "double edged sword of the Word," and cut ourselves loose from the mess of the past. You simply cannot receive nutrition from the things that you left when Jesus set you free. Maybe that is the reason you don't have victory. On Sunday morning you can shout, speak in tongues,

125

and run up and down the aisles. By Monday night you're sitting naked on a folding chair in front of a computer screen trying to pull up some kind of pornography and wonder why you don't have victory! You cannot continue to feed yourself the garbage from where God called you out of, and you cannot receive strength from what you were delivered from. As a matter of fact, once a woman has a baby, all that is inside of her has to come out or it will kill her.

Entrance into the kingdom is like a birth. Jesus said to get into my kingdom you have to be delivered from where you came from, and you have to cut loose from what used to feed you nutrition. The problem for many is trying to be in the kingdom, while at the same time not cutting the cord of the past.

Once a baby is born it has to be cleaned up... *"Neither wast thou washed in water to supple thee; thou wast not salted at all, nor swaddled at all."*

I will never forget the excitement I felt when we found out my wife was pregnant. It was late February and she was 2 1/2 weeks past the due date. We had gone to the church that morning and when we returned to the apartment I noticed she didn't look right. I said, *"What's wrong?"* She replied, *"I think I'm having contractions."* Now the doctor already told us when the contractions were one hour apart we needed to head to the hospital. So, we started timing and driving all at the same time. By the time we got to the hospital the contractions were one minute apart!

126

Now I had prepared myself to go to the delivery room. I watched all the informational things I knew you had to watch – I watched soap operas.

I watched them because somebody is always pregnant on the shows. I mean, let's get real, you can watch a certain soap opera for a year, stop for five years, and when you come back to the show nothing has really changed. The woman that was pregnant five years ago just had the baby when you started watching it again.

Have you noticed that all the doctors were handsome, and caring just like Marcus Welby M.D.? The mother looked like Jennifer Aniston, and the father like Brad Pitt. All the nurses looked like Dallas cowboy cheerleaders. You go into the delivery room and everything is beautiful. There is no mess, no tension and everyone is so happy. Even the mother and daddy are smiling. What a beautiful picture. The TV doctor holds up the TV baby in front of the TV camera. The TV baby looks like the Gerber baby. He has a beautiful complexion, a head full of hair, and looks like he weighs 30 pounds. This is what I was expecting – **BUT, HOLLYWOOD HAS LIED TO US!**

When I went into the delivery room, my wife wasn't smiling. As a matter of fact, she had a look on her face that said, *"If I could get my hands around your throat I would choke your eyeballs out of your head!"* The nurses were sweet and kind, but I have to tell you they didn't look like the Dallas Cowboy cheerleaders, they looked like the Dallas cowboy players. Big girls. Being the loving and caring husband that I am I tried to encourage my wife. I bent down and said, *"Baby it's okay, breathe."* To which she said, *"SHUT UP!"* I was ready for this to be over.

Dr. Simmons cut the umbilical cord, handed me the baby and said, *"Congratulations, it's a boy."* I looked down to see this beautiful Gerber baby, but instead I saw something I did not recognize. I said to myself, *"Dear God, what is this I am looking at?"* He was purple, that's right purple. He had blood all over him. It was under his fingernails, up his nose, in his ears, and in every pore. He was a nasty mess. When Dr. Simmons saw me crying he must've thought I was overjoyed at being a father. I was holding this little bundle of a mess and crying and I shouted a prayer, *"Dear God, I will have to spend $1 million in plastic surgery before I can take this kid in public."* God I don't know what I'm going to do? I was praying hard, breaking every curse I could think of. I think at one point I shouted *"I bind this thing by the power of the Holy Ghost. Whatever curses have been passed on, I repent in Jesus name."*

Finally, the doctor said for me to hand the baby back to the nurse. I said another quick prayer and asked God to give the nurses wisdom to fix this thing. The nurse took him and the transformation began.

They cleaned him up. Sucked out all the blood, cleaned out his fingernails and ears. They washed him all over, wrapped him up in a blanket, put a cool hat on his head, and brought that pretty little rascal back to me. I looked down and said, *"Everything is going to be all right now."*

You see my friend, there was nothing wrong with my son. He just looked like what he came out of!

What we have been trying to do is to get people delivered (born again), and we expect them to look like the Gerber baby. The truth is when they come through the doors they are going to look like and smell like what they came out of. It is our job to take the water of the Word, clean them up and make them productive citizens of the Kingdom of God. Millions of people are born of the will of God and have the right to become sons and daughters of the kingdom, but many remain infants, and refuse to grow up into mature sons. The right to become an overcomer is there, but tragically few do so.

*"**Thou wast not salted at all.**"* That statement makes no sense to us unless you understand childbirth in biblical times. In those days they would take a baby for the first eight days after it was born and pack them in salt. They did not have prenatal vitamins, and all of the things we have today to keep a baby healthy. Theologians tell us only 23% of all infants born in biblical times made it out of infancy. They packed them in salt to toughen them up. If you didn't, or if you mishandled the baby, they could get what was called "bruised blood" that would lead to an infection and the baby would die.

We are called "salt." Why? Because we are birthing babies into the kingdom. The problem with many people is they never got salted, or toughened up. They are easily offended and upset just like a baby (1 Corinthians 3:1 – 3). Our churches are filled with spiritual infants who need to grow up. I don't mind feeding babies a bottle but when you have to spread the whiskers to slip in the nipple, well, enough is enough.

"But thou wast cast out in the open field, to the lothing of thy person, in the day that thou wast born. And when I passed by thee, and saw thee polluted in thine own blood, I said unto thee when thou wast in thy blood, Live; yea, I said unto thee when thou wast in thy blood, Live."

Here's a baby. The umbilical cord is not cut. It has not been cleaned up, salted, or wrapped up. It's cast out into an open field dying. God looks at it and says**, "LIVE."** I would rather have one word from God than 10 million dollars, wouldn't you?

One word from God can change every circumstance you are in right now. Ezekiel continues to prophesy and says, "*I have caused thee to multiply as the bud of the field, and thou hast increased and waxen great, and thou art come to excellent ornaments: thy breasts are fashioned, and thine hair is grown, whereas thou wast naked and bare.* Do you know what he is saying? You are filling out, you are becoming a woman. God always symbolically likens the church to a woman. He stated, *"You are growing up, and becoming a mature woman. You are producing milk to birth more babies."* The reason why most churches never birth any babies is because there is no milk to be found. When God's people begin to mature God says**, *"Now I*** *can send you babies because I know they are not going to starve to death!"*

Over the entrance to the Kingdom of God is a door marked, *"Enter by The New Birth."* It's the only way, there is no other. Even though He only talked about it one time to a man at 3 o'clock in the morning, Jesus told Nicodemus unless a man is born again of the water and the Spirit he cannot **SEE or ENTER INTO The Kingdom of God.**

For those of us who have been born again we already know we have been delivered from the kingdom of darkness and transferred into the Kingdom of God's beloved son (Colossians 1:13). It's like entering into the atrium or lobby of the huge building with hundreds of rooms. You can stay in the lobby and truthfully say, *"I am in the building."* You can even brag about how beautiful and how well appointed the place is. But, if you don't open all of the doors that are available to you and discover Kingdom wealth you will forever live the life of a spiritual infant – and that my friend is a tragedy!

The Word of God is like a seed, when planted in the human heart it has the supernatural ability to impregnate and produce a harvest.

The very first parable Jesus preached was about the ability of the "seed." (See Mark 4:3–20). When a lost man repents of his sin, and invites the Lord Jesus to forgive him he is born again by the Word of God (the seed) and by the Spirit of God!

Without seed there isn't any life. But, without the proper soil there will be no fruit. In the next chapter were going to look at the first parable Jesus taught. In the parable of the **"Sower and the Seed"** Jesus explained there were four categories of people who hear The Word of the Kingdom. Those who hear the word are compared to dirt. Only one response produces lasting fruit. Which one are you?

Turn the page and find out "What Kind of Dirt You Are?"

Chapter 8

BREAK UP YOUR FALLOW GROUND

The same day went Jesus out of the house, and sat by the sea side. And great multitudes were gathered together unto him, so that he went into a ship, and sat; and the whole multitude stood on the shore. And he spake many things unto them in parables, saying, Behold, a sower went forth to sow; And when he sowed, some seeds fell by the way side, and the fowls came and devoured them up: Some fell upon stony places, where they had not much earth: and forthwith they sprung up, because they had no deepness of earth: And when the sun was up, they were scorched; and because they had no root, they withered away. And some fell among thorns; and the thorns sprung up, and choked them: But other fell into good ground, and brought forth fruit, some an hundredfold, some sixtyfold, some thirtyfold. Who hath ears to hear, let him hear. Matthew 13:1-9

Opposition was building. The spirit of antichrist was fast at work. The opposition of the scribes and Pharisees, the religious leaders of the day, were leading the charge. Somehow, someway He had to be stopped (12:14). Remember, the spirit of religion will always oppose the Kingdom of God. The Pharisees loved to play the "gotcha" game. It seemed every time Jesus turned around the religious crowd was watching and waiting for Him to break one of their precious rules. After all, they are the protectors of the law. It was their job to make sure that everyone stayed in line. Like a snake, they were waiting in the weeds ready to deposit their poison.

The "gotcha game" is still being played today. These modern day "turf shepherds" are nothing more than first century Pharisees wrapped up in a spirit of religion. They come at you with pious platitudes, but when they open their mouth the sharp teeth of a wolf is exposed. I am not saying everyone who goes to church, or is in a leadership position is a Pharisee – not at all. But, backbiting, gossiping, and splitting a fellowship of genuine believers is not what I would call a New Testament Church.

I grew up in a religious, legalistic church. All I heard was "God is going to get you for that! He is going to come and smite you big time." Listen my friend, God is not trying to sneak up on you and catch you doing something bad so He can send you to hell. That's not the God who really is, or the God I know. That's religion, and it is right out of the pit of hell!

REMEMBER THE CONTEXT

To better understand Matthew 13 you need to remember the context of what had already taken place. The teaching of the parables in chapter 13 is not an isolated event.

Matthew 11-14 consists of a 24 hour period in the life and ministry of Jesus. He and his disciples already had four confrontations with the scribes and Pharisees.

- The Pharisees accused His disciples of breaking the Sabbath. 12:1-5.
- On the same day Jesus entered a synagogue and healed a man with a withered hand. The Pharisees again accused Jesus of breaking the Sabbath. 12:9-13.
- Jesus healed a man possessed by a demon. The

Pharisees accused Jesus of casting out demons by the power of the chief demon, Beelzebub. 12:22-30.

- The Pharisees changed tactics, and asked Jesus for a sign. As if healing a man's hand, and casting out a demon so that a blind mute man can both see and speak wasn't enough. Jesus did not mince words, He simply rebuked them! 12:38.

Obviously I just gave you the highlights. Read it for yourself and you will even see Jesus' mother and brother's show up to try to take Him away (Verses 46-50). I don't know, maybe they were trying to stop him from causing any more problems. Whatever the reason, Jesus simply said,

"For whosoever shall do the will of my Father which is in heaven, the same is my brother, and sister, and mother."

CAN YOU HEAR ME NOW?

But, in Chapter 13, Jesus' ministry reaches a turning point. He starts to speak to the crowds in parables. At first the disciples didn't get it. They were confused, and wanted to know why He spoke in parables?

And the disciples came, and said unto him, Why speakest thou unto them in parables? He answered and said unto them, because it is given unto you to know the mysteries of the kingdom of heaven, but to them it is not given. For whosoever hath, to him shall be given, and he shall have more

abundance: but whosoever hath not, from him shall be taken away even that he hath. Therefore speak I to them in parables: because they seeing see not; and hearing they hear not, neither do they understand. And in them is fulfilled the prophecy of Esaias, which saith, By hearing ye shall hear, and shall not understand; and seeing ye shall see, and shall not perceive: For this people's heart is waxed gross, and their ears are dull of hearing, and their eyes they have closed; lest at any time they should see with their eyes and hear with their ears, and should understand with their heart, and should be converted, and I should heal them. But blessed are your eyes, for they see: and your ears, for they hear. For verily I say unto you, That many prophets and righteous men have desired to see those things which ye see, and have not seen them; and to hear those things which ye hear, and have not heard them. Matthew 13:10-17

Jesus did not speak in parables because he wanted to purposely confuse or condemn people. These "earthly stories with heavenly meanings" would open the understanding of those who had "ears to hear," but would bring hardness to the hearts of those whose understanding was darkened. It wasn't that God did not want the Pharisees and other doubters of Jesus to hear and understand. It was the result of their hard hearts, closed ears, and blind eyes. They didn't get it because they didn't want to get it. The same is true even today!

These stories were no ordinary stories. Jesus actually calls them "mysteries of the kingdom." You might be thinking,

Brother Caldwell, if he is speaking in a mystery how in the world can we understand it?

I am glad you asked. I am not going to revisit chapter 6 again except to remind you that "mysteries" are understood by Divine revelation. They reveal inside information Jesus did not reveal to anyone except those with trusting and searching hearts. Is it possible the reason most church people don't understand the message of the Kingdom is that they are spiritually deaf? Jesus made it plain if you have ears to hear you can understand the mysteries of the kingdom. *"Who hath ears to hear, let him hear."* (13:9).

I am amazed at people who say they are "born again" by the Spirit of God and yet have no desire to know the mysteries of the kingdom. These mysteries are the deep things of God hidden from the foundation of the world (13:35), and are now available to those who are willing to search them out (Proverbs 25:2).

I hear people say, *"Oh Brother Caldwell, I want all God has for me. I want to go to the next level of anointing and revelation."* Yet, those same people would rather go to a ballgame, or stay at home and watch reruns of *Leave It to Beaver* than attend one of a meeting where the message of the Kingdom is being preached with the power of the Holy Ghost. Nothing wrong with a ballgame, or watching television, that's not the point. The point is – how much revelation are you willing to dig for?

A casual approach to the mysteries of the kingdom will

never increase your understanding. Jesus gave a simple but profound way to the *"principle of increase."*

It's pretty simple really; the more you want, the more you will get. But, if you don't use what you have you will lose it. **"For whosoever hath, to him shall be given, and he shall have more abundance: but whosoever hath not, from him shall be taken away even that he hath." (13: 9)**

Instead of digging into the word for revelation our churches are filled with people who have "dead ears." The writer of Hebrews used the word *"dull"* to describe people who should have been mature enough to teach the word, instead they were still in the first grade reciting their ABC' s.

Of whom we have many things to say, and hard to be uttered, seeing ye are dull of hearing. For when for the time ye ought to be teachers, ye have need that one teach you again which be the first principles of the oracles of God; and are become such as have need of milk, and not of strong meat. Hebrews 5:11-12

The word *"dull"* is a Greek word meaning "*slow, or sluggish."* It is used to describe a numb limb, like an arm or a leg. If you have ever had the experience of sitting in one place too long (like on an airplane) you know what it's like to stand up and your leg won't move. It is sound asleep! You can scream at it, speak in tongues over it, and declare it awake in the name of Jesus. But, until you start moving, and get the blood flowing no amount of wishing and hoping is going to wake it up.

The spirit of deafness is rampant. If we are going to be led by the Spirit of God, we must learn to recognize His voice, and to do that we must learn how to hear. As a child of God, you have experienced the new birth. You have the Holy Spirit living inside of you. And to top it off you are a citizen of the Kingdom. You have the privilege and right to hear His voice. Jesus said in John 10:27: *"My sheep hear my voice, and I know them and they follow me."*

This is not the first time we have been instructed to hear:

Isaiah 55:1-3*: Ho, every one that thirsteth, come ye to the waters, and he that hath no money; come ye, buy, and eat; yea, come, buy wine and milk without money and without price. Wherefore do ye spend money for that which is not bread? and your labour for that which satisfieth not? hearken diligently unto me, and eat ye that which is good, and let your soul delight itself in fatness. Incline your ear, <u>and come unto me: hear, and your soul shall live</u>; and I will make an everlasting covenant with you, even the sure mercies of David.*

You find the word "hear" 19 times in Matthew 13. The first three Gospels gave us the parable of the Sower, and in each one the imperative to "hear" is different. It does matter that we hear God's word, because *"Faith cometh by hearing, and hearing by the word of God* (Romans 10:17).

Jesus said, in Matthew 13:9*, "who <u>hath</u> ears to hear let him hear."* In Mark 4:24 He said, *"Take heed <u>what</u> you hear."* And, in Luke 8:18 He said, *"Take heed <u>how</u> you hear!"*

139

BACK TO THE PARABLE

The very first parable Jesus taught was about the ability of the "seed." (Also see Mark 4:3 – 20). When a lost man repents of his sin, and invites the Lord Jesus to forgive him he is born again by the Word of God (the seed) and by the Spirit of God!

I love the way Jesus tells a simple story out of the common culture to reveal a divine mystery. As He sat in the boat looking over the crowd no doubt there were farmers, fishermen and herdsmen listening to His words. He talked about something they could all relate to.

WHAT DOES IT MEAN?

Without seed there isn't any life. But, without the proper soil there will be no fruit. Jesus explained there were four categories of people who hear *The Word of the Kingdom.* Those who hear the word are compared to dirt. Only one response produces lasting fruit.

A sower goes out to sow seed. A farmer knows in order to get a harvest he has to plant seed. A wise farmer will broadcast a generous amount. Some of the seed falls on a well-traveled path, some on rocky ground, and some among thorny weeds. But, some falls on good soil, the kind necessary for a huge harvest.

- The seed that falls on the well-worn path just lies there. In and around the farmer's fields were paths packed down hard because of so much foot traffic. Because of the hard ground seed remained on top, and became a quick lunch for the hungry birds.

- The seed that falls on the rocky ground doesn't have enough good soil for deep roots. The blazing sun comes out, and of course it shrivels up and dies.
- The seed that falls among the thorny weeds sprout, but eventually the weeds suck up all the water and chokes the tender plants before they have a chance to produce.
- Only the seed that lands on good soil produces a harvest. But, as Jesus explained even the harvest size varies. Some will yield 30x, others 60x, and others 100x. It's not so much about the size, but the fact that the soil produced something.

Let's look at the three elements:

1. The Sower is Jesus.

In explaining the parable (versus 18-23) Jesus does not say He is the one sowing the Word of the Kingdom. But, if you read on in the chapter I believe He gave us the answer in the parable of the wheat and tares (13:36-43), when he said, *"The one who sows the good seed is the Son of Man..."* We have no reason not to believe that this is true for this first parable also.

Everywhere Jesus went He generously sowed the seeds of the Kingdom. Like a good farmer He scattered seed everywhere, not holding back. He demonstrated there was no seed shortage in the kingdom of God. He wanted a bountiful harvest. And, in order to do that He knew He had to sow generously.

Jesus demonstrated the Kingdom of God is ever increasing, and in His kingdom there is abundance. The King is more than capable of taking care of His citizens. All you have to do is read the Sermon on the Mount.

Jesus encouraged His hearers not to worry about anything (Matthew 5:24 – 34). That included the physical, emotional, and spiritual needs of those who are a part of His kingdom. No one is turned away. For example, there was enough to feed 5,000 men, plus women and children. I think you get the point -there is never a shortage of anything in the Kingdom of God.

So, the sower is extravagant, and the seed is abundant.

2. The Seed is the Word of the Kingdom.

This is not just the written word, the Bible, although it would be included in the "Word of the Kingdom." The Greek word is "logos" or "word." *Strong's concordance says it is – "speaking to a conclusion" – a word, being the expression of a thought; a saying. It is preeminently used of Christ (John 1:1), expressing the thoughts of the Father through the Spirit."*

The message of the Kingdom was delivered in words, which are like seeds that have the miraculous, mysterious power to multiply. The Word of God is "living and powerful" (Hebrews 4:12). The Word has life giving power, and that power is imparted to those who will receive it and believe it.

The "Word" of the Kingdom is what Jesus came to

deliver. When He came to this planet, the Word was made flesh (John 1: 14). Isaiah prophesied of the event, and said in chapter 9:6, ***"For unto us a child is born, unto us a son is given: and the government shall be upon his shoulder:***

When the Word (Jesus) arrived on this planet He brought the kingdom and everything it included. He did not bring salvation, or a rapture plan. He did not just bring a blueprint for the New Jerusalem. He did not just bring divine health and healing. What He brought was a governmental system that included all these things and more. He brought God's government "upon His shoulder." The "increase" of His government will never end (Isaiah 9:7). He did not come to make converts, but citizens and ambassadors of the Kingdom. He did not come to start a new religion, but to take back Kingdom rule and authority.

3. We Are the Dirt

The seed is the word of the Kingdom. The various kinds of soil are the various kinds of people who hear the word of the Kingdom. The harvest is limited only to one kind of response. It is the person who hears, understands and bears fruit. To receive an abundant harvest the seed must take root and be cultivated.

It's a shock to the system to realize that three-fourths of the seed did not bear fruit-

A. Hard Heart.

And he spake many things unto them in parables,

143

saying, Behold, a sower went forth to sow; And when he sowed, some seeds fell by the way side, and the fowls came and devoured them up: Matthew 13:3-4

When any one heareth the word of the kingdom, and understandeth it not, then cometh the wicked one, and catcheth away that which was sown in his heart. This is he which received seed by the way side. Matthew 13:19

You have an enemy. His strategy is to take the "Word" as soon as possible. He does not want it to have a chance to germinate. The evil one knows if you wake up and embrace the word it will produce fruit. If he leaves the word of the Kingdom without snatching it away, it will have a result.

You can take the best seed in the world, but if it does not have good soil nothing will be produced. If you don't believe me try taking seed and sowing it on your carpet in your living room. It may look good but I can promise you it won't produce a harvest!

A hard heart needs to be broken up. Hosea declares in 10:12, *"Sow to yourselves in righteousness, reap in mercy; break up your fallow ground: for it is time to seek the Lord, till he come and rain righteousness upon you.*

What does it mean to break up your fallow ground? The word "break' comes from a Hebrew word called *"Shaw bar"* and means *to crush, to burst, and to tear into pieces.* The statement *"Fallow Ground"* is ground (heart) that at one time was fruitful. It is ground that at one point in time had been cultivated and

144

productive, but now it is just dirt. There are many who sit in the pews on Sunday who were once on fire for God. Whenever they talk, they talk of past glory. They think because they were on fire for God twenty years ago it's still true today. The telltale sign of a Pharisee is they are more interested in what God did in the past, and they despise what God is doing today. The spirit of religion will always despise the plow.

Well, Brother Caldwell what can we do? It's simple. To break up fallow ground you have to plow it. You may not want to hear this but many people run from the plow. Why? The plow will dig deep, turn the soil, and break up the clumps of hardened dirt. The plow will expose everything under the surface. If there is something there that doesn't belong it will be exposed. Take my word for it the plow will disrupt your comfort zone! Once the plow has turned over the ground (the heart) new seed can be planted.

B. The Shallow Heart.

Some fell upon stony places, where they had not much earth: and forthwith they sprung up, because they had no deepness of earth: And when the sun was up, they were scorched; and because they had no root, they withered away. Matthew 13:5-6

But he that received the seed into stony places, the same is he that heareth the word, and anon with joy receiveth it; Yet hath he not root in himself, but dureth for a while: for when tribulation or persecution ariseth because of the word, by and

145

by he is offended. Matthew 13:20-21

He is not talking about soil that has rocks in it, but of a shallow layer of soil on top of solid rock. Because of the underlying rock the plant is unable to put down deep roots. There are some who received the Word with joy, and then when persecution and pressure come they wilt. Sun represents persecution that comes because of the Word of the Kingdom.

Sunshine is a good thing, and necessary for growth. But, when the root system is shallow it will kill a plant instead of helping it to grow.

The Word of the Kingdom has to be more than surface dressing. Emotion does not produce fruit. Now, don't get me wrong, I'm not against the emotional part at all. I love to preach in meetings where people shout, and get excited about people being healed. But, emotion can never replace weak faith, or an insincere commitment. Emotion is no substitute for "fruit", and prayer is not a substitute for righteous action.

Beneath the shallow layer of soil lies the hard rock of an indifferent spirit. The cost of discipleship in time, effort, and commitment is too high. What starts out as a "big bang" of Amen' s and Hallelujahs ends up in a fizzle of "so what."

The layer of rock under the surface must be "busted up." Until that happens the shallow root system will continue to die under the scorching heat of pressure, trials and tribulations.

Is not my word like as a fire? saith the Lord; and like a

hammer that breaketh the rock in pieces? Jeremiah 23:29

C. The Crowded Heart.

And some fell among thorns; and the thorns sprung up, and choked them: Matthew 13:7

He also that received seed among the thorns is he that heareth the word; and the care of this world, and the deceitfulness of riches, choke the word, and he becometh unfruitful. Matthew 13:22

There is nourishment for thorns, and nourishment for wheat, but not enough for both. The same is true in life. Some hear the Word, understand it, but are distracted by the cares of the world. The worries of life overpower the promises of God. When we are more occupied with the "things" of this world than the "things" of God we are in danger of being unfruitful and unproductive as far as the Kingdom is concerned.

"And the deceitfulness of riches..." The word deceit means the "distortion of truth for the purpose of misleading." It literally means to look for something in the wrong place. Once again I remind you, if the devil cannot distract you with an evil ambition, he will try to distract you with a righteous one.

I made a statement in a sermon a few months ago. I said, *"I would rather have one Word from God than ten million dollars."* After the service someone came up to me and said, *"Caldwell, you don't like money very much do you?"* Don't you love it when people take your words and twist them to mean something totally different? That's not what I meant at all!

Jesus said it is the *"distortion of truth for the purpose of misleading that is the problem."* It is the *"love of money that is the root of all evil"* (1 Timothy 6:10). I don't love money itself, I love what it can do for the Kingdom. Money has no morals, it is amoral. Money takes on the personality, and values of the one holding it. There is no such thing as righteous money or unrighteous money. In the hands of a righteous man it can do righteous things for the kingdom of God. In the hands of an unrighteous man it can do horrible and despicable things for the kingdom of darkness.

I can promise you one thing, if you spend your life chasing after money, you will never catch it. Instead of pursuing money, pursue the things of God. Become a seed sower (2 Corinthians 9:6 – 11), and you will never have to worry about "things" (Matthew 6:33).

D. The Fruitful Heart.

But other fell into good ground, and brought forth fruit, some an hundredfold, some sixtyfold, some thirtyfold. Matthew 13:8

But he that received seed into the good ground is he that heareth the word, and understandeth it; which also beareth fruit, and bringeth forth, some an hundredfold, some sixty, some thirty. Matthew 13:23

But, then there are those who hear, understand, and

produce a harvest of fruit. Not all produce the same; some 30, some 60, and some of 100 fold. When a tiny seed is placed in good soil a miracle takes place. The farmer knows inside that seed is a promise. The promise is; *"plant me and I will produce thousands more just like me."* I am told if a farmer planted enough seed to grow 1.4 million plants (that is about 1 acre of wheat) his efforts will yield 77,300,000 kernels. Now, that is seed power to the max!

It's all about the fruit. Jesus knew most people would not receive His message of the Kingdom and bear fruit. His intention was never to attract large crowds to win their favor. He knew it was possible to have shallow roots of belief and yet not be saved (John 2:23-25). The bottom line is this – unless fruit is produced, there is no saving faith in the heart!

The true test of salvation is fruit. Jesus said in Matthew 7:20, **"Wherefore by their fruits ye shall know them."**

What we need in the body of Christ are more fruit inspectors. Jesus said we can know a great deal about a person by examining the fruit in their life. The word *"know"* is the Greek word *"epignosis,"* which is a compound of two words, *"epi"* and *"gnosis."* The word *"epi"* means *"upon."* The word *"gnosis"* means *"to know,"* and is the Greek word for *"knowledge."* The two words together form the word that means, *"to come upon or to happen upon some kind of knowledge and carries the idea of making a discovery."* There is no doubt you can make quite a discovery by simply examining and observing the lives of people. In reality, actions do speak louder than words!

The Bible gives us different kinds of fruit:

- The fruit of holiness (Romans 6:22).
- The fruit of Christian character (Galatians 5:22–23).
- The fruit of good works (Colossians 1:10).
- The fruit of winning others to Christ (Romans 1:13).
- The fruit of sharing (Romans 15:25–28).
- The fruit of praise (Hebrews 13:15).

I am sure there are those who would say, *"Wait a minute Brother Caldwell, the Bible says we are not to judge."* Actually it doesn't say that at all! Jesus said in **Matthew 7:1-2... *"Judge not, that ye be not judged. For with what judgment ye judge, ye shall be judged: and with what measure ye mete, it shall be measured to you again."***

It just says that if you are going to step into the place of judgment and judge somebody else's motives you better be prepared for judgment to come back to you. There is a big difference between spiritual discernment and judging someone to condemn them.

You have to remember Jesus was surrounded by the scribes and Pharisees who were guilty of false judgment. They had convinced themselves of their own righteousness and were convinced everyone else was unrighteous. They were hypocrites and Jesus exposed them!

We have to use Holy Ghost discernment. If you accept

everyone who claims to be more than they really are you are in for a big time heartache. Let's face it my friend not everyone is a sheep who claims to be. As one old-time preacher used to say, *"Just because we're the Lord's sheep does not mean we should let people pull the wool over our eyes!"*

If you want a productive fruit filled life then prepare the soil of your heart. Put down deep roots so that you can navigate through life's pressures. While at the same time allow the Holy Ghost to shine the light of the Word on any weeds that might stifle growth. Pursue spiritual riches and run from the deceitfulness of worldly wealth. Make sure the soil of your heart is ready to receive the Word of the Kingdom.

BREAK UP YOUR FALLOW GROUND!

And when you do these things Jesus said you can expect a harvest that is both marvelous and miraculous!

Chapter 9

TWO OF THE DUMBEST THINGS I EVER HEARD

(IN CHURCH)

And when he was demanded of the Pharisees, when the kingdom of God should come, he answered them and said, The kingdom of God cometh not with observation: Neither shall they say, Lo here! or, lo there! for, behold, the kingdom of God is within you. Luke 17:20-21

Please do not misunderstand the title of this chapter. I am in no way inferring everything I learned in church was dumb. Nor, am I referring to any particular person.

You need to understand my background. I was raised in an old-time Pentecostal church. I thank God for my upbringing. I am proud to say my daddy (who was the preacher) made sure his boys were in church every time the door opened, but I have to admit the only thing I really knew about God was he was mad all the time. I mean, if I thought something was fun God thought it was bad. He had no sense of humor at all. This attitude was very confusing to me as a child because my family was, and is today a fun loving bunch of folks.

The picture I had in my mind was God was like a policeman standing on the corner watching and waiting for us boys to mess up. I thought He would grab us, hit us on the head with a Billy club, and send us straight to hell. I can still remember hearing sermons about the rapture of the church. We were told, *"He's coming like a thief in the night at the midnight hour!"* Of course, my brothers and I would take that literally. After service we would run home jump in bed and sweat it out. We kept our eyes on the clock. At two minutes till midnight we pulled the covers up over our heads and held our breath. We just knew as soon as the clock struck twelve Jesus would come back and we would be left behind. But, as soon as we heard dad snoring in the next room, and it was two minutes after midnight, we knew we had a 24 hour grace period. We dodged another bullet! That was nothing more than the spirit of religion instilling fear in our hearts.

If you were not raised that way, you really can't relate to what I'm talking about. But, trust me on this, whatever background you have more than likely at some point you were given a similar picture of God. Whether we want to admit it or not, most of us are products of who taught us, and what our cultural environment told us was right and wrong.

The point is this; there a lot of things being preached and taught in church that are more from personal preferences, cultural traditions, and just plain old *"That is what I've always heard,"* than the clear teaching of the Word of God. I think it's about time we stopped reading into the Bible and start reading out of the Bible!

It does matter who you allow to teach you. Jesus condemned the Pharisees for their false teaching. He said they were ***"Blind leaders of the blind. And if the blind lead the blind, both shall fall into the ditch"*** (Matthew 15: 14).

For example: if you have been taught by someone who mistakenly believes the stripes of Jesus can no longer heal, then it will be hard to receive healing. The same is true about understanding the principles of biblical prosperity and kingdom economics. If the one teaching you believes you are more spiritual if you live in poverty, then it will be more difficult to believe God wants you to live in prosperity.

We are never called to be disciples of anybody except Jesus, or anything except the Kingdom of God (Matthew 10:24-26). I think it's about time we stopped being disciples of a certain man, or a particular group. If I call myself a disciple of a specific denomination, or particular brand of teaching I will never fully understand the mysteries of the kingdom. They actually may be teaching truth, but from my experience, it is only one piece of the truth, not the whole. We can certainly learn from others. We need to learn how to be disciples of the King himself. Maybe we ought to be spending more time reading the "red print" and less time following after the latest fad.

The mysteries of the kingdom are reserved for those who will *"hear and understand."* Jesus said in Matthew 15:10, ***"And he called the multitude, and said unto them, Hear and understand:"*** In Mark 4:23 He puts it this way, ***"If any man have ears to hear, let him hear."*** He was not talking about just the physical aspects of hearing.

Jesus was constantly speaking on two levels. One, to the natural ear, and the other to the spiritual hearing of those who were sitting in front of Him. The Greek word for "hear" is *"akouo"* which means *"to hear with understanding."*

Once I learned what Jesus was talking about, I understood how it's possible for two people to be sitting in church, but hear differently. Both hear the same message about the Kingdom of God, but one walks away with new understanding and a deeper commitment to the King, while the other walks away without any change at all. One heard with understanding (which produced change), while the other refused to allow the "seed" of the kingdom to take root in the soil of his heart.

Jesus said in John 8:32, ***"And ye shall know the truth, and the truth shall make you free."*** Does that mean all I have to do is read the Bible and I will be free? Yes and no – it's important to read it, but it isn't the "truth" that you read about that sets you free, but it's the truth you know or better yet "understand" that sets you free. *Known truth produces change.*

When you were young and your mother pointed to the hot stove and said, *"Now baby the stove is hot, don't touch it. It will burn your hand."* No doubt your little mind knew that statement was true. When you got close to the stove you could feel the heat. You could see the flame. But, if you decided to test your mother's word and touch the stove then you had an "understanding" of the truth – *"Ouch that hurt!"*

You can know a lot of things without understanding. For example: You can know the truth of Romans 8:28, ***"And we*** *know that all things work together for good to them that love God, to them who are called according to his purpose."* But, you will never have an understanding of that verse until you are in a situation of tragedy or desperation, and then when the Holy Ghost shows up to guide and comfort you. That is when the Scripture becomes real.

SPEAKING DUMB THINGS

There are seven chapters in Luke (13-19) that consist of one day in the ministry of Jesus. As always, He is preaching about the kingdom of God. The events are not isolated, but connected, so you have to read them in context. Time and space will not allow me to point out everything in these seven chapters. But, two events jumped off the page and grabbed my attention. Now, I don't want you to be upset, but when I show you these two things you're going to instantly recognize them. Why do I say that? Because, you have probably heard these things all of your life.

I call them "dumb things" because if you dig into the Bible you discover not everything we have been taught is true.

For generations we have sat on pews on Sunday morning like little birds waiting for the mama bird (the Pastor) to chew up our food and regurgitate it into our mouths. Now, that may sound disgusting to you, but it is a spiritual fact. Many (not all of course) pulpits in America have become nothing more than "echoes" repeating the same old message. For some, it is easier to preach messages out of old commentaries than to get on their face with nothing but the Bible and receive a "now" word from God. We are called to be and "voice" not an "echo." The echo of today's gospel has become a syrupy, cotton candy message that makes you feel good, but doesn't change anything.

If you want to challenge me on that statement, then I would ask you to look around and tell me if things are getting better or worse? Has the modern church made any impact on society? You don't have to be a brain surgeon or a rocket scientist to figure out things are not looking too good right now.

Iraq is all but lost. Afghanistan has become a nightmare. North Korea is flexing its nuclear muscles. China is buying up America and holding us hostage with our debt. Mexico, Guatemala, and Honduras are invading our southern borders not with troops and guns, but with children. Whether we like it or not America has become a debtor nation.

On the home front the welfare state continues to grow. All the while the average American citizen looks around and says *"I don't recognize my country anymore."* From the White House to the church house things are a mess.

I am convinced the only change agent is the Gospel of the Kingdom. We don't need more churches. If an abundance of churches would have saved the planet then this planet would have been saved two generations ago. No, that is not the answer.

God give us more Joshua's who are not afraid to lead their people to claim the promised land of this generation. Canaan is not a picture or type of heaven. I don't want to burst your bubble, but when the people crossed over Jordan there was an enemy on the other side. Yes, it's true, the land was theirs by inheritance and covenant. But, they could not enjoy the abundance of the land until they strapped on weapons and took it! There is no war, fighting, or territory to be taken in heaven. The land of Canaan is the picture or type of the promises of God, and abundant living. It may sound sweet to sing about, *"That golden shore on the other side of Jordan,"* but it's just not a true picture. Here's a thought – maybe we should stop getting our theology out of the hymn book and start reading the Bible again.

Elijah told God (while hiding in a cave) he was the only one left that cared anything about the truth. He must have been shocked when God told him He had thousands more just like him. This is a generation of "no names" who are coming out of the cave. These cave dwellers are unafraid to stand up and declare the Word of the Kingdom. They would rather suffer the persecution, criticism, and pressure of being a "voice" than climbing the denominational ladder of success as an "echo."

They know the culture around us will never change until we stop regurgitating slop and start declaring the Kingdom of God is here! They refuse to sit down, backup, or shut up.

Take a deep breath, the air is about to get thin.

Dumb Thing #1 – <u>The Kingdom Is Reserved for the Future, not now.</u>

And when he was demanded of the Pharisees, when the kingdom of God should come, he answered them and said, The kingdom of God cometh not with observation: Neither shall they say, Lo here! or, lo there! for, behold, the kingdom of God is within you. Luke 17:20-21

When I talk about the present reality of the Kingdom I have to be careful because there is a theological scam going on. It has been around for years. It's called *"Kingdom Now"* theology. This teaches, among other things, *"The kingdom is here now, this is it. There Is no Heaven or Hell."* The "Kingdom Now" teaching is without Biblical foundation. It is being driven by fear and the skill of profane religious snake oil salesman to pump up a crowd in a false anointing. All it takes is a few keystrokes on your computer and you can find out the real truth behind this false teaching.

The Pharisees basically said, *"You have been talking about the kingdom, so where is this kingdom you have been talking about?"* The constant theme of His ministry was to talk about the Kingdom. Jesus had a single focus, **"Repent: for the kingdom of heaven is at☐hand" (Matthew 4:17).** Preaching about the kingdom of God was not just the first thing He preached, but it was the only thing He ever preached publicly. You just had to figure at some point they were going to ask Him about it, and that's what they did in verse 20.

The Jews were taught from the first moment they could read about the coming of the kingdom. For centuries they looked and longed for the coming One who would break the yoke of oppression. But, their patience was wearing thin. Their land was occupied by foreign conquerors. All they heard was, *"One day God is going to crush the Romans like He had done with foreigners in the past."* Then Israel would be established as the political head of the world and they would all enjoy prominent positions in this promised kingdom. The big misunderstanding of those around Jesus was that the Kingdom of God is a future kingdom and that it is entirely an earthly visible kingdom.

The Pharisees were convinced Jesus was just another in a long line of phony Messiah's. They said, *"You keep talking about the Kingdom, but you don't look very much like a King. And if you are a King where is your Kingdom?"*

You can always tell when the Pharisees were around because they only want to talk about the past, but never the present. The King standing before them did not look like a King according to their tradition. The Kingdom had arrived but it didn't look like the Kingdom they were expecting. Their conclusion was this so-called King was a fake and a fraud.

Once again Jesus destroyed their misconceptions and traditions: ***"The kingdom of God cometh not with observation: Neither shall they say, Lo here! or, lo there! for, behold, the kingdom of God is within you."***

It's not coming with signs to be observed. By the way, that is not a future tense but a present tense. He is not talking about the future coming of the Kingdom. The present reality of the Kingdom is not seen in a geographical location. It is not about a visible throne, a mighty army, or an established

Parliament.

He put the kingdom within us (Romans 8:15-16). It is found in its Sons, Citizens, and Ambassadors. There will be an establishment of a physical kingdom in the future, but what Jesus is talking about is His government displayed in the hearts of His people, now, not some future Millennial Reign.

The response of Jesus revealed the fact they did not have a clue. The King was standing in front of them, and yet they missed it by hundred miles.

They had the same problem Nicodemus had in John 3. I talked about it in chapter 7 so I won't repeat it all here, but just to remind you Jesus told Nicodemus, ***"Truly, truly I say to you, unless one is born again, he cannot see the Kingdom of God.*** The word *"see"* means to *"perceive or to know."* Unless you are born again you don't know that the Kingdom actually exists. Later in the conversation Jesus added this...***"Except a man be born of water and of the Spirit, he cannot enter into the kingdom of God.*** The word "enter" does not mean to "go to," it means to *"enjoy the benefits of."* Nicodemus before you can *"perceive or know the Kingdom, and enjoy its benefits, you must be born again!"*

If you haven't been recreated, if you haven't been raised from the dead, if you haven't had the blinders taken off, if you don't have new life, you can't see the King or enjoy the benefits of the Kingdom. And He went on to say, ***"You must be born of the water and the Spirit,"*** *that's spiritual birth cleansing by the*

power of God and be given His Holy Spirit, or you'll never see
the Kingdom...never.

It's past time for us to stop living with the definition of the Kingdom given to us by the Pharisees. The Pharisees (the spirit of religion) are the same yesterday today and forever. Unless they are born again, their message will always be the same, it never changes.

We need to realize the Kingdom of God is the government of God operating now in those who have a relationship with the King, whose name is Jesus. You will find in this Kingdom, which is operating today, an abundance of: wealth and prosperity, peace and joy, complete and total health, and victory over the kingdom of darkness. How are you going to beat a deal like that!

Dumb Thing #2 – Jesus Was Poor and Rich People Can't Go To Heaven.

In my early years I had the impression if you had any wealth at all you were not very spiritual. So, if you had any success or received any material blessings you were just flat out backslidden. Most of the time when people don't want to talk about money is because they don't have any.

In the church I grew up in you just didn't talk about money unless it was about tithing. But, to be honest it was more like paying protection money to the mob than giving out of the cheerful heart to the work of the Lord. Pay your money, on time, and if you cheat God is going to get you!

162

By and large the Church has bought into it, and that is one of the dumbest things I've ever heard!

The Scripture used to justify rich people can't go to heaven is found in Luke 18:18-27:

And a certain ruler asked him, saying, Good Master, what shall I do to inherit eternal life? And Jesus said unto him, Why callest thou me good? none is good, save one, that is, God. Thou knowest the commandments, Do not commit adultery, Do not kill, Do not steal, Do not bear false witness, Honour thy father and thy mother. And he said, All these have I kept from my youth up. Now when Jesus heard these things, he said unto him, Yet lackest thou one thing: sell all that thou hast, and distribute unto the poor, and thou shalt have treasure in heaven: and come, follow me. And when he heard this, he was very sorrowful: for he was very rich. And when Jesus saw that he was very sorrowful, he said, How hardly shall they that have riches enter into the kingdom of God! For it is easier for a camel to go through a needle's eye, than for a rich man to enter into the kingdom of God. And they that heard it said, Who then can be saved? And he said, The things which are impossible with men are possible with God.

Jesus did not tell the young man to get rid of all of his stuff so he could be saved. The issue was not salvation but his relationship to material things. The young ruler told Jesus he obeyed the law. Jesus said that's great. Your mouth is telling me one thing, but your money is telling me something else!

163

Ecclesiastes 10:19 says, *"A feast is made for laughter, and wine maketh merry: but money answereth all things."* That verse does not say money *IS* the answer to all things. If money is the answer to all things then Jesus is unnecessary. The word *"answereth"* means to *"speak, or to testify of a certain thing."* Your money sings, it shouts, and it testifies about what you value and love. Obviously, this young man who came to Jesus had money testifying about what his priorities were. Jesus put his finger on this young man's spiritual pulse. Money was an issue and had to be dealt with. As far as I know this is the only time someone walked away sadly after an encounter with Jesus.

So I was told that Jesus said if you are rich you cannot enter the kingdom of God.

Here's the issue. Can a man be saved, go to Heaven when he dies, and still not enjoy the benefits of Kingdom living in the here and now? Yes, I believe so.

First of all, there is a difference between the **KINGDOM OF HEAVEN** and the **KINGDOM OF GOD**. The Kingdom of Heaven is a physical location with a street of gold and walls of Jasper. The **KINGDOM OF GOD** is within you. It is God's government and rule in each individual life.

He is not saying rich people cannot go to Heaven. The Bible is clear. Anyone, rich or poor, who confesses Christ as Lord, and repents of their sin is born again (Romans 10:9-13).

For example: Here is a man who made his fortune by operating in the world's system. He hears the message of

164

salvation and gives his heart to Jesus. Jesus said unless that man changes his mind and begins to operate in kingdom principles he will never enjoy all the benefits of the Kingdom of God (verse 25).

Through the years I have met many men of wealth. They were good and sincere men who loved Jesus. I found some trusted in their wealth more than trusting God to take care of them. If you have wealth you have to be very careful not to allow riches to be a substitute for an intimate relationship with the Holy Ghost. Riches have a way of distracting from the important things of the Kingdom (1 Timothy 6:6-11; 17-19). The more you think you have to lose the greater the resistance to the kingdom!

*"**For it is easier for a camel to go through a needle's eye, than for a rich man to enter into the kingdom of God.**"*

The eye of the needle is not referring to a sewing instrument. I believe it referred to something they would understand. You see, in those days cities had gates. During the day the gates would be opened for travelers to come in and go out. At night, for protection against thieves, the gates would be closed. The "eye of the needle" would be a small gate in the larger gate that travelers or merchants would have to use if they wanted to enter after dark. The camel could only enter by being led unencumbered and crawling on its knees.

Jesus meant exactly what He said. It is difficult for someone who is comfortable and has need of nothing to suddenly put God first in his life. Because their wealth becomes their "god." The disciples were amazed at Jesus' statement and asked, *"Who then can be saved?"* Jesus then told them*, "With men this is impossible; but with God all things are possible" (Matthew 19:26).*

God is the prime factor who makes everything possible. With God in our lives, even the impossible becomes possible. Without God, no one has a chance to enter or enjoy the benefits of the Kingdom of God. You might as well try to pass a camel through the *"eye of a needle."*

Was Jesus poor?

See if this statement sounds familiar? *You shouldn't have money because after all Jesus was poor. You shouldn't have any material wealth because Jesus didn't have any.*

To prove the point Jesus was poor half of 2 Corinthians 8:9 is quoted; *"Yet for your sakes he became poor."* You might want to read the whole verse- *"Though he was rich, yet for your sakes he became poor That ye through his poverty might be rich."*

When did Jesus become poor? Jesus became poor on the cross when He willingly gave up EVERYTHING so you and I might become rich IN ALL THINGS.

At the cross a covenant exchange took place:

- I exchanged my unrighteousness for His righteousness.
- I exchanged my sickness for His wholeness.

- I exchanged my poverty for His riches.
- I exchanged my fear for His peace.
- AND SO MUCH MORE!

Some have even painted the picture of Jesus as a homeless person pushing a shopping cart down the streets of Jerusalem collecting bottles and cans. Bless His heart, poor Jesus had no place to sleep, and no money to buy food. If He were walking the earth today no doubt he would be on welfare, standing in line waiting for a free phone from the government.

If you go by the way Jesus is portrayed in many denominations He was some kind of limp wristed religious fanatic who was scared of his own shadow. If you believe that I don't know what you are going to do when Jesus "meek and mild" grabbed a whip and destroyed the tables of the money changers in the temple. Doesn't sound very meek or mild does it?

The main focus of His teaching was the Kingdom of God (Matthew 6:33). The core of that teaching was about money and our stewardship of material things. Jesus talked more about money than He did Heaven and Hell combined. 11 of 39 parables talk about money and stewardship. 1 of every 7 verses in the Gospel of Luke talks about money. About 800 Scriptures deal with the subject of money. Seems odd for a man who supposedly had no money to talk about it all the time. Jesus was not broke, busted or disgusted!

You know Brother Caldwell the Bible said Jesus didn't have a place to live... **And Jesus saith unto him, "The foxes** *have holes, and the birds of the air have nests; but the Son of man hath not where to lay his head." Matthew 8:20*

Sad to say I bought into that. Then I decided to read the Bible for myself. I discovered Jesus had a house. He was not homeless. Why would He invite them to "come and see," If He didn't have a place to stay?

And the two disciples heard him speak, and they followed Jesus. Then Jesus turned, and saw them following, and saith unto them, What seek ye? They said unto him, Rabbi, (which is to say, being interpreted, Master,) where dwellest thou? He saith unto them, Come and see. They came and saw where he dwelt, and abode with him that day: for it was about the tenth hour. John 1:37-39

Jesus had no money. Is that true? Again, I decided to read the Bible for myself instead of believing what I was told.

The Bible says Mary and Joseph sacrificed two turtle doves which is a poor household's sacrifice according to the law (Luke 2:22-24; Leviticus 12:2-8). That proves He was poor. Really? When He was dedicated at the Temple he was eight days old. But, something is going to happen that will change everything.

The wise men showed up. There wasn't just three of them. These Magi traveled from Babylonia (the region of modern day Iran and Iraq) in large numbers. According to Arabic history they normally traveled in a group of a minimum of 40 up to 70.

So, we have a group of at least 40 showing up, not at the stable where Jesus was born, but when Jesus was almost two years of age. It wasn't just three of the wise men giving Gold, Frankincense, and Myrrh. They all gave. As I often say – they loaded them down with enough so that Mary and Joseph took Jesus on a two-year vacation to Egypt!

When they saw the star, they rejoiced with exceeding great joy. And when they were come into the house, they saw the young child with Mary his mother, and fell down, and worshipped him: and when they had opened their treasures, they presented unto him gifts; gold, and frankincense and myrrh. Matthew 2:10-11

When Jesus died they gambled for his robe. Do you know why? Jesus wore a seamless robe, the most expensive suit of the day. I doubt anyone would gamble for an old worn out rag, but they might over an expensive seamless robe. To put it in modern terms Jesus wore an "Armani" suit, and they don't come cheap!

Then the soldiers, when they had crucified Jesus, took his garments, and made four parts, to every soldier a part; and also his coat: now the coat was without seam, woven from the top throughout. They said therefore among themselves, Let us not rend it, but cast lots for it, whose it shall be: that the scripture might be fulfilled, which saith, They parted my raiment among them, and for my vesture they did cast lots. These things therefore the soldiers did. John 19:23-24

If you don't have any money you don't pay taxes, right? Jesus paid his taxes, therefore he had income. Money was not a problem for Jesus! He never worried about money or paying bills. There is no scripture telling how Jesus stayed up at night trying to figure out how to operate his ministry!

Notwithstanding, lest we should offend them, go thou to the sea, and cast an hook, and take up the fish that first cometh up; and when thou hast opened his mouth, thou shalt find a piece of money: that take, and give unto them for me and thee. Matthew 17:27

Not only did Jesus pay taxes but obviously he had enough money to require a treasurer. Admittedly, the treasurer (Judas) was a thief and a traitor. But, it doesn't take away from the fact the ministry of Jesus had money to operate.

This he said, not that he (Judas Iscariot) cared for the poor; but because he was a thief, and had the bag, and bare what was put therein. John 12:6

Maybe you are thinking: *"Brother Caldwell, I don't want a lot of money, it will change me."* Money does not have the power to change anybody. Money is neutral and it takes on the character of the hand that's holding it. Money doesn't shape character it reveals character. If you are a cheapskate now without money, guess what you will be if you get lots of money? You're right – a rich cheapskate!

It's time we changed our "stinking thinking" about money. How many have bought the line if God wanted me to have lots of money He could drop it on my front doorstep? Only one problem with that – there is no money in heaven. Not one American dollar, British pound, Mexican peso, or even a Japanese yen. Money is the currency of earth, not Heaven. Honor is the currency of Heaven, but it takes money to operate on this planet.

If you think money is so evil then the next time your boss hands you a paycheck give it back. Just tell him money is evil and you don't want that filthy stuff around your house. If poverty is what God wants for you, and you think it makes you more spiritual, then give away your car, sell your house and live under a bridge!

On the other end of the spectrum are those who go in the super spiritual direction. They say money is not important. It doesn't mean anything to them at all. They will just live *"by faith,"* which for some means, *"I would rather live off of somebody else. It's too unspiritual to work and earn money to feed my family."*

If you think money is not important, then the next time your house payment is due just send in your coupon with a note. Tell your mortgage lender that you have prayed about it and you don't feel "led" to send any money this month. Tell them not to worry about it, maybe next month the Lord will lead you to send a payment. How long do you think that would last before they foreclose on your house? Normally about three months.

The next time you buy groceries go to the cashier and tell

them *"thank you for the food"* and walk out. How far would you get before you were sitting in the back of a police car? By the way, I hear they have a lot of free stuff down at the county jail – three meals a day, and a real cool orange jumpsuit.

Wake up! It takes money to live in our society. It takes money to operate ministry. It takes money to establish the covenant.

But thou shalt remember the Lord thy God: for it is he that giveth thee power to get wealth, that he may establish his covenant which he sware unto thy fathers, as it is this day. Deuteronomy 8:18

Believing that poverty is Godly is really just an excuse for people who have not prospered according to God's plan of economy (Luke 6:38). Prosperity is not so that we can just hoard money and things, but rather so that we can become a conduit of God's blessings, both spiritual and financial.

And God is able to make all grace abound toward you; that ye, always having all sufficiency in all things, may abound to every good work: 2 Corinthians 9:8

Only the spirit of religion can get you to believe poverty is a blessing, and prosperity is evil. Only tradition can convince you God is after your money, and any preacher who talks about money is a crook. The Bible never, ever teaches such a foolish notion. God does not want, or need your money, what God really wants IS YOU!

Now that's some the dumbest things I've ever heard!

Crazy teaching and dumb things would clear up in a heartbeat if one issue was settled – **WHO IS YOUR KING?** It is either King Jesus or Satan, not both. The question has been and continues to this day *"Who is calling the shots in our life?"* Once kingship is established everything else falls into place.

In the next (and final) chapter we will determine the central issue of KINGSHIP!

Chapter 10

WHO IS YOUR KING? (Who's Your Daddy?)

Now when they had passed through Amphipolis and Apollonia, they came to Thessalonica, where was a synagogue of the Jews: And Paul, as his manner was, went in unto them, and three sabbath days reasoned with them out of the scriptures, Opening and alleging, that Christ must needs have suffered, and risen again from the dead; and that this Jesus, whom I preach unto you, is Christ. And some of them believed, and consorted with Paul and Silas; and of the devout Greeks a great multitude, and of the chief women not a few. But the Jews which believed not, moved with envy, took unto them certain lewd fellows of the baser sort, and gathered a company, and set all the city on an uproar, and assaulted the house of Jason, and sought to bring them out to the people. And when they found them not, they drew Jason and certain brethren unto the rulers of the city, crying, These that have turned the world upside down are come hither also; Whom Jason hath received: and these all do contrary to the decrees of Caesar, saying that there is <u>another king, one Jesus</u>. Acts 17:1-7

How would you feel if you had received an invitation to speak in a strange city to a group of people you had never met? You were asked to speak for three sessions. The subject matter you chose to speak about was *"the Kingdom of God."* After the third session you walk outside and a large crowd had gathered. By the look on their face they were not happy. When they see you they begin to chant, over and over, *"Troublemaker, leave our city!"* You are exasperated. You find the ringleader of the mob, and ask him why they think you should leave? His reply was a shocker. He said, *"We don't want you here. What you are teaching is upsetting our city. You are teaching things contrary*

174

to our culture. If you don't leave we will have to take action!"

No, that did not happen to me, (at least not yet), but it did happen to the apostle Paul and his team in the city of Thessalonica.

Paul would always find his way to the local synagogue. And, when given the opportunity to preach, his message was simple and to the point... ***"Opening and alleging, that Christ must needs have suffered, and risen again from the dead; and that this Jesus, whom I preach unto you, is Christ.***

Why were they considered troublemakers? What was it about the message he preached that caused them to accuse him of *"turning their world upside down?"* It seemed wherever Paul and his team landed one of two things happens – a revival or a riot – most of the time both!

You don't have to read very far to discover the answer. He was accused of teaching ***"there is another king, one Jesus."***

They were bringing something new to the culture. The issue was not one of religion – or even a new religion. It is just like today. You can pick your favorite religion on any given Sunday. If you don't like the one on this corner, you can find another one across the street. We are better than Baskin-Robbins because we have more than 31 flavors!

Later on when Paul showed up in Athens he was deeply disturbed. ***"Now while Paul waited for them at Athens, his spirit was stirred in him, when he saw the city wholly given to*** *idolatry (17: 16).* Not wanting to offend, or leave anyone out, they even had an altar dedicated TO THE UNKNOWN GOD (Verse 23).

You might say the Greeks and Romans were god poor. The Romans were famous for their gods. The apostle Paul lived in a world known for its idolatry. Worshiping many gods was normal. It was not the exception, it was the rule.

For example:

- Saturn: One of the oldest gods, who was once the ruler but his place was taken by his son Jupiter.
- Jupiter: The god of the sky, and considered the most important.
- Juno: She was Jupiter's wife.
- Neptune: Jupiter's brother and the god of the sea.
- Minerva: The goddess of wisdom.
- Mars: The god of war.
- Venus: The goddess of love, and the lover of Mars.

Well Brother Caldwell I am so glad we live in world where we don't have to worship all those crazy gods!

Before you get too excited about that let me give you my definition of an idol – **"It is anything you have to check with before you will obey the Holy Spirit."** We are not that much different from the early Romans and Greeks. Our idols just have different names.

In our culture we don't worship Greek gods. We worship

at the altar of sports, work, pleasure or anything that can grab our attention and passion. We will criticize a church for spending money on outreach to the city, while at the same time weep with joy when our favorite sports figure signs a contract for one hundred million dollars. We gripe and complain when the pastor stands up on Sunday morning to take an offering, but have no problem dropping twenty thousand dollars on a new boat. We mock those who get too excited on Sunday morning, and yet have no problem losing our voice yelling for our favorite team to score another touchdown on Saturday.

We have even found a way to worship the different seasons of the year. How many times have I heard someone say, *"You know in the summertime we spend a lot of time on the lake, we don't have time to go to church. After all, we can worship God at the lake just like we can at church."* Sounds so spiritual doesn't it? Sure, you can worship God anywhere. The truth is you don't go to the lake to worship God – you go to fish, waterski, and just have fun. And, there's nothing wrong with any of it, except when we use it as an excuse for unfaithfulness. Why don't we just call it what it is instead of trying to make it sound like something it's not?

The real issue in Paul's day was not, do you have religion? Everybody did. No, the bottom line issue was, "who is your King?" Why were they so upset when Paul declared the reality of King Jesus? To recognize another king besides Caesar was a dangerous proposition. Paul didn't teach another religion, he taught another culture with a different King. And, His name is Jesus not Caesar!

He was living in an environment saturated with "Caesar worship." The worship of the emperor was above all the other gods. Caesar represented the State, and the State was the King. Whoever was the "Caesar" at the time was to be worshiped as God. You can burn incense at the temple and you are free to worship at the altar of Mars or any of the other gods. But, when it comes to the real issues of life, including the economy, the State knows best. Neptune may get your incense and sacrifice, but Caesar got your taxes!

ARE THE TROUBLEMAKERS TODAY?

Paul wasn't considered a troublemaker because he organized a protest against the local temple. He didn't hold secret meetings with union leaders trying to get better wages. He did not hide behind the cloak of religion to launch a campaign for social justice. He didn't do any of those things. He just introduced them to a new King who left the unseen world to introduce to the seen world the message of reconciliation.

Nobody wants the title of troublemaker, right? After all, we had been told to be wise as serpents, harmless as doves. We have a tendency to major on the "harmless" part. Don't rock the boat. Just stay in your pew, sing your little choruses, and occasionally shout hallelujah. I think we have mastered the art of "be nothing, say nothing, and do nothing." We have turned the powerful message of the Kingdom of God into a lightweight, minimum impact nothing of a religion. I even heard about a mega church who told its staff never to mention the name Jesus on Sunday morning for fear of offending non-Christians. Really? Yes, really.

The modern day "cotton candy" message doesn't have enough power to blow the dust off of a gnat's wing! The feel-good gospel will never change our culture. Whatever you do don't go outside the four walls of your church and declare to a culture totally given over to idols – THERE IS ANOTHER KING, AND HIS NAME IS JESUS!

We have become thermometers instead of thermostats. A thermometer will tell you what the temperature is. But, a thermostat will tell you what the temperature is going to be based on the instructions you give it. A thermometer only reflects, while a thermostat regulates. I'd rather be a thermostat any day, wouldn't you?

They were accused of *"turning the world upside down"* (Verse 6). The message of the Kingdom won't turn the world upside down, it will turn the world right side up!

Jesus did not come to preach religion or to establish Christianity. His message was***..."Repent, for the kingdom of heaven is at□hand"*** (Matthew 4:18). He called his message the Gospel of the Kingdom. It is the only thing Jesus ever called the Gospel.

His mission was to ***"seek and to save that which was***

lost" (Luke 19:10). It says to, *"Save that which was lost," not "them."* We have misinterpreted that verse for centuries. He declared He had been sent by God for the purpose of preaching the kingdom, **"I must preach the kingdom of God to the other cities also: four therefore I am☐sent." (Luke 4:43).**

Brother Caldwell are you suggesting that we stop preaching about salvation and the Cross of Jesus? NO – I have said it before, and I will say it again NO that is not what I am saying! What I am trying to communicate is the preaching of the Kingdom of God contains all of that and more. But, any preaching of the Gospel of salvation that does not include the Gospel of the Kingdom is totally inadequate.

Paul, in his farewell address to the elders of Ephesus said*: "But none of these things move me, neither count I my life dear unto myself, so that I might finish my course with joy, and the ministry, which I have received of the Lord Jesus, to testify <u>the gospel of the grace of God</u>. And now, behold, I know that ye all, among whom I have gone preaching <u>the kingdom of God</u>, shall see my face no more.*

*Wherefore I take you to record this day that I am pure from the blood of all men. For I have not shunned to declare unto you <u>all the counsel of God</u>. (Acts 20:24-27).** You don't have to be a Bible scholar to see Paul equated the Gospel of God's grace with the proclamation of the Kingdom, and in so doing considered it the complete "counsel of God."

Jesus came to earth to take back what Adam lost in the

garden – not salvation, but dominion. Adam did not fall from heaven, he fell from his position as CEO of the third rock from the sun! God gave Adam authority and dominion over the planet, and Adam gave it away (Genesis 3:1-7).

The culture of the kingdom of God is a direct contradiction to the kingdom of darkness. Jesus came to replace the existing world order of darkness with God's order of light. The kingdom of God is "knowledge" and the kingdom of darkness is "ignorance." No amount of darkness can extinguish the light of the kingdom of God. John declared in chapter 1 of his Gospel, *"In him was life; and the life was the light of men. And the light shineth in darkness; and the darkness comprehended it not.* The literal translation is *"the darkness can never extinguish it!"*

THE ISSUE IS VERY PERSONAL

When I declare my King I am declaring I will live by His culture, which includes His standards of economics. When Jesus said, *"repent,"* He meant change your mind and your way of thinking. The old pattern of accepted behavior in the kingdom of darkness is to live life your way. When a man repents he is giving up all of his old arguments with God and changes the direction of his life. Repentance is not a one-time experience at the altar. Repentance is not determined by how many buckets a man can fill with his tears. It is an ongoing attitude of submission to the King.

The new way of behavior is to recognize He is the King of every aspect of my life. The *"new wine"* of the kingdom lifestyle will never fit into the *"old wineskins"* of the past (Matthew 9:17).

As a citizen of the kingdom of God you and I enjoy rights and privileges. Along with privileges comes responsibility. We are responsible to live according to the laws of the kingdom. The pattern of acceptable behavior is found in the kingdom manual – it's called the Bible! Our wonderful King tells us all through the manual how to live, prosper and enjoy all of the full benefits of the kingdom.

When you pick up the kingdom manual you discover a beautiful promise In Jeremiah 29:11 – ***"For I know the thoughts that I think toward you, saith the Lord, thoughts of peace, and not of evil, to give you an expected end."*** The King has declared a great plan for each of us. We serve a King who is dedicated to our prosperity, protection, and peace. He is totally committed to provide an expected end for each of us.

How can you tell who is the King of your life?

At least two ways:

1. By what you worship.

I love the story of Mary and Martha. We can learn from both of them. They are both found in the church today, and I meet them all the time.

The background of Mary and Martha is found in Luke 10:38-42:

182

Now it came to pass, as they went, that he entered into a certain village: and a certain woman named Martha received him into her house. And she had a sister called Mary, which also sat at Jesus' feet, and heard his word. But Martha was cumbered about much serving, and came to him, and said, Lord, dost thou not care that my sister hath left me to serve alone? bid her therefore that she help me. And Jesus answered and said unto her, Martha, Martha, thou art careful and troubled about many things: But one thing is needful: and Mary hath chosen that good part, which shall not be taken away from her.

The problem Martha had was not that she was working in the kitchen, not at all. The problem was the spirit of the kitchen was working in her. You have heard it said, *"All work and no play makes Jack a dull boy,"* but I say unto you, *"all work and no worship makes Jack dry of soul, and just plain miserable!"*

Don't be too hard on Martha. First of all she is found in every Church, and we need her. Her gifting and zeal are invaluable. But, what happened to her has happened to thousands of Christians, including many of those in a leadership position. She got out of balance, her attitude was affected, and she could no longer see what was really important in the life of the Spirit.

Verse 38 says, *"Martha welcomed Him into her home."* Don't think for a minute that she was one of those who just tolerated Jesus. She was one who wanted Him in her home. The home of Mary and Martha, along with their brother Lazarus, was a home Jesus loved. It was a place of peace, rest and refreshment.

Verse 40 says she "got distracted with much serving". Martha fell into the same trap so many fall into. She was out of balance, and could not see Jesus for all those pots and pans! If we are not careful we might end up like Martha. We can become so busy in ministry the vision of the King is obscured by the heavy load. Martha was removed from His presence (vs.39), so she not only had trouble "seeing Him" but also "hearing" Him!

Jesus said, *"Come unto me, all ye that labour and are heavy laden, and I will give you rest. Take my yoke upon you, and learn of me; for I am meek and lowly in heart: and ye shall find rest unto your souls. For my yoke is easy, and my burden is light (Matthew 11:28-30).* If your burden is not light, it's not from God.

If you go into the modern Church on Sunday morning it is like going into the kitchen of a cafeteria at the local mall. Loads of activity, with lots of noise, with people hurrying around, all in the name of trying to get the food line stocked. After all, we want everyone to have a choice of what they want to eat. The Pastor becomes the main Chef, trying to serve up something that won't give the congregation indigestion! The theme of the Modern Church ought to be - *"Let's Just Rattle Those Pots and Pans."* Sad to say in most Churches you couldn't hear God if He wanted to say something for all the noise. Remember it was to the Church at Ephesus Jesus said, *"I know your works, and your labor",* but He also said *"you have left your first love".*

Martha had upside down priorities. ***Verse 40 says she told the Lord, "bid her therefore that she help me."***

She was upset and feeling so alone, just like Elijah (1Kings 19:4). She was filled with a complaining Spirit. Show me someone who is always complaining, and I'll show you someone who doesn't understand who they are in Christ. They act more like slaves than sons.

Well Brother Caldwell I guess what you are telling me is I just need to stop doing anything for the Lord and take a break from ministry. Right? No, that's not what I'm telling you at all. That's going to the other extreme, which is just as dangerous. I've met plenty of people whose attitude is, *"I am saved and all I want to do is just Praise the Lord, go to conferences, follow my favorite teacher around the country, and bask in the heavenly glow 24/7."*

How would your boss feel if you went into his office every day and told him how much you loved him and you just want to sit in his presence all day? Forget about going out and doing the job you are paid to do. I doubt you would last very long before you were shown the door. It doesn't work that way in the kingdom either.

WHERE'S MARY?

Mary discovered the balance.

Luke 10:39*: "who also sat at Jesus' feet and heard His word".*

Luke 10:42*: "But one thing is needed, and Mary has chosen that good part".*

Here is a lady with a different spirit altogether. She is sitting at his feet. I'm told in that culture you sat at someone's feet for two reasons: one is to learn and the other is to worship. Maybe the reason we don't sit at His feet more often is we are afraid of what we might hear! Let's face it, isn't it more comfortable for us just to get busy, and not have to deal with such issues than spending time with Him?

Every time we see Mary in Scripture she has found a way to worship. After the death of her brother (John 11) Mary fell at His feet and learned Jesus is the *"Resurrection and the Life."* If you are going to have a funeral, Jesus is the best person in the whole universe to invite. He never met a funeral he didn't like – death could not stay in his presence.

Follow her into John 12 and see her spirit of worship continue. *"The house was filled with the odour of the ointment" (Verse 3).* In case we were wondering if the worship of Mary was just an isolated affair watch what she is doing here. She anointed His feet with a pound of ointment of spikenard. Some have suggested the ointment was worth one year's wages; others say it was her inheritance. Whatever the case I believe it represented all that she had. Her worship filled the room with its odour!

2. By whom you obey.

The Kingdom is not a democracy. There are no votes taken in Heaven! There are only two potential Kings: King Jesus, or Satan. Whoever gets my vote is the one in charge. It's all about control. The issue is *"Who is calling the shots in my life?"*

It is not enough for a man to say I believe in Jesus and nothing else is needed. Obedience to His word always follows genuine belief. Singing "I'll fly away," is not enough to change the culture. When the Kingdom of God is reduced to something you inherit in the "Sweet By and By," it becomes irrelevant to the issues we face today.

I remind you Jesus did not die to take back God's power. He never lost it. He came to restore and take back authority. Power is not authority and authority is not power. Power and authority are governmental twins. Power exercised without authority is morally wrong. Authority without the power to back it up is worthless.

FINALLY

If you know me very well you know I don't like cold weather, and I especially don't like snow. Several years ago I was in Colorado preaching at a tremendous church with a great man of God. After the Monday night service I came outside and it was spitting snow. I said, *"Lord, please don't let it snow. You know I have to leave here and drive to another city on Wednesday night, and the last thing I need is a pile of snow. If you love me at all I'm begging you please don't let it snow!"*

187

I got up the next morning and apparently He didn't love me as much as I thought because the ground was covered. The snow hurt the crowd a little but we still had a great meeting. On Wednesday night, after the last service, I told my daughter, *"Tomorrow morning we're going to get up and get out of here. We have a two hour drive to the next meeting and I don't want to get snowed in."* A two-hour drive turned in to almost nine hours. Needless to say I was not very thrilled!

We arrived at the next location, and I was holding my breath praying for the snow to go away. The host pastor decided it would be a good idea to take me up to the ski slopes in Vail. For some strange reason he thought it would be exciting to show us some sites. I am sure some people would love it, but I have to confess I hated every minute of it. The wind was blowing, and it was so cold all I could do was shiver. I said to myself, *"Self, tomorrow I'm getting out of here."*

It was Friday morning and the pastor knocked on the bedroom door at our condo and said, *"Brother Caldwell, we have a problem. A blizzard has hit."* He wasn't kidding. I looked out the window and decided the tribulation had taken place and we missed the rapture. Snow was so deep all you could see was the top of my rental car. I decided to do the only thing I knew to do, and that was to dig out my car and head south. No matter what it took I'm getting off this mountain!

We finally made it to Interstate 70. They shut down the freeway, and I am stuck. We sat in the car for four hours waiting to go. Finally, they said the freeway was opened. I made it is far as the left-hand turn to jump on the interstate and I was stopped again. I looked over and saw these little orange cones standing between me and my next preaching assignment. I thought to myself, *"Those things are not made out of metal, they look like soft rubber. I could run them over, and even if they get stuck under my car eventually they will come loose."*

Before I made my decision to make a run for it this police lady walked by my car. So I rolled the window down and I asked her if we could go. She said, *"We are working on it."* She probably came by my window about eight or nine times. And, each time she would say the same thing, *"No, not yet."* You know you can think about some strange things when you feel trapped. One time when she came by I kind of sized her up. She probably didn't weigh more than 135 pounds and after all I had been working out. I'm strong so I think *"I can take her."* I thought I could probably whip her if I needed to. I have power in the engine of this car to run over those rubber cones and if she tried to stop me, well like I said, she doesn't want to mess with me today!

Here's the problem. I had all the power I needed, but she had something I didn't have. A little shiny badge on her shirt that gave her authority. She may have been little, and yes I probably could have taken her, but then I would have to deal with the full force of the Colorado State Police. You see, she had the authority and the power to back it up. Finally, she came over and said,

"Sir, it is open now you can go." She walked over and moved those little rubber cones. She just simply waved me onto the interstate. Do you know what happened? She released the authority, and when she turned loose of the authority I turned loose of the power!

Jesus Christ came to reestablish authority on this planet. He has released the flow of authority through His body the church. The sad part is most of the church does not even realize the authority to bind and loose is our privilege and right to enforce. Authority in the kingdom is a flow. When you are under authority it flows through you. When you move out from under authority the flow stops (Matthew 8:5 – 13).

We exercise and operate in the flow authority by the words of our mouth. Once you open your mouth and call those things which are not as though they were God exercises power to back up the word. God is just sitting in Heaven with the engine running waiting on us to open our mouth and declare the word of the Kingdom. Our words propel Heaven into action!

If you forget everything I have written about the Kingdom of God, please remember these 5 important truths:

1. The Kingdom is ever present. It is here and it is now.

2. The Kingdom is ever increasing and expanding, not decreasing.

3. The Kingdom has everything you need for abundant living. There is no lack or shortage in the Kingdom.

4. You don't enter the Kingdom through membership, but through birth.

5. Jesus is coming back, but not until *"The Kingdom shall be preached in all the world for a witness unto all nations; and then shall the end come."*

IT IS TIME TO:

- **<u>Enjoy</u> your fellowship with the Father. You are a <u>son</u>.**

- **<u>Embrace</u> your rights and privileges in the Kingdom. You are a <u>citizen</u>.**

- **<u>Exclaim</u> the message of the King. You are an <u>ambassador</u>.**